Life

Mastery

Life
Mastery

*Challenging
Your Impostor*

*Embracing Your
Genuine Self*

Sally Fisher

CROWN PUBLISHERS, INC./NEW YORK

Published by Crown Publishers, Inc., 201 East 50th Street, New York, New York 10022. Member of the Crown Publishing Group.

Random House, Inc. New York, Toronto, London, Sydney, Auckland

CROWN is a trademark of Crown Publishers, Inc.

Manufactured in the United States of America

LIBRARY OF CONGRESS CATALOGING-IN-PUBLICATION DATA
Fisher, Sally
    Life mastery: challenging your impostor, embracing your genuine self / by Sally Fisher.—1st ed.
    1. Self-actualization (Psychology) 2. Visualization (Psychology) 3. Authenticity (Psychology) 4. Impostor phenomenon. I. Title.
    BF637.S4F57   1993
    158'.1—dc20   93-4331
                                                                    CIP

ISBN 0-517-58943-5

10 9 8 7 6 5 4 3 2 1

FIRST EDITION

To my children,
Fisher Stevens, Tracy Fisher, and Julie Fisher,
and to the memory of friends who have died in the era of AIDS

Contents

Acknowledgments

I want to thank the many Masters who have contributed to my personal growth and to the process of creating Life Mastery. Some are included within these pages. My teachers have come from every walk of life and have followed many paths. Primary among them are the courageous and compassionate men and women whom I've encountered working within the worldwide AIDS/HIV community. Those facing their mortality and those standing with them have illuminated the infinite possibilities that life offers.

I also want to thank those who have brought support, encouragement, and reality to the writing of *Life Mastery*. Thank you to Peter Ginsberg, my agent, who decided that I should put what I knew on paper and became my first guide. Thank you to my editor, David Groff, who was able to amplify my personal voice and give rhythm to my silent song. Thank you to Paul Monette, who made it all seem real. And thank you to Philip Lynch, who has made room in his life for this work.

Introduction

Introduction

Ultimately, if I follow my heart I am on the right track. I always know what is best. I just get talked out of it by almost anyone or anything that I look to for guidance. I always think someone else has the answer so I always seem to find myself back on the recovery treadmill, staring into another abyss. I've followed something other than my heart and I have to start the learning process all over again.

Stephen Tutt, *Los Angeles, 1986*

THIS IS A BOOK ABOUT LIFE MASTERY. Mastery is not an obscure or esoteric process reserved for a few select souls. It is practical and possible. With Mastery you can become the author of your life rather than a character at the mercy of its plot. Mastery means that you discover who you are and trust yourself—your Genuine Self, not the Impostor who for too long has dominated you. Mastery means that the circumstances no longer dictate the quality of your life. You can become connected to your personal power as well as your spiritual source.

Most of us have spent our lives in a quest for the essential, Genuine Self. If you have been attracted to this book it is likely that you have been on this quest. You may have been helped along the way by what we refer to as self-help books and seminars. While I mean this book—and the process of Life Mastery—to show you something new and more powerful, I recognize the value of what you may already have learned.

There is a lot of information available today. We have moved beyond blaming the unhappy seeker for his or her own fate. We are even beginning to move beyond seeing ourselves as victimized by our parents and society, though these are clearly the roots of our issues. We have been offered the bigger picture by great thinkers such as

Alice Miller, who broke with the traditional systems of psychoanalysis, publishing many books that are accessible to laypersons, the best known of which is *Drama of the Gifted Child;* and Pia Melody, who did cutting-edge work in defining family systems and codependency. We have come to understand the cycle of abuse and dysfunction that we have grown up with, and to see how we fit within that cycle. We have developed entire new languages to explain the plight of the individual adrift in the sea of denial and self-deception.

Yet we still seem to be adrift.

We live in the era of recovery, the era of the inner child, the era of reclaiming our malehood, femalehood, and personal space. The era where we decided we could change our lives by changing our thoughts, by retraining, by dancing rituals in the moonlight, or by hugging teddy bears. We've renounced our parents, forgiven our perpetrators, and joined support groups. We've gone through transformational experiences. We've gone through metaphysical phases. We attend all manner of self-help workshops, gatherings, and twelve-step meetings. We grow obsessed with gurus, culture heroes who seem, at least briefly, to have all the answers. We've gone through boxes of tissues and lots of money—but too many of us have not genuinely found ourselves. We search relentlessly for what we think we want, which is the truth, and we will do anything to find it—except think for ourselves.

The search for a better and more coherent way to live your life may leave you feeling as though you are just spinning your wheels. It is as if you are addicted to the process. Hooked on the search for your lost self. The search is more familiar than your Genuine Self—who has slipped away in the process of growing up. But if you want to you can find yourself again—and begin the process of Life Mastery.

The self you've lost is the person you were when you came into the world. The core of who you really are became the object of the search because you began to separate from it shortly after your birth. Your separation from your Genuine Self begins as the input from the outside world invades your boundaries and violates the sense of safety and well-being that is necessary for you to grow up with a powerful sense of self-love and worth. Among the first lessons you learn about yourself from the world around you is that you are flawed; the more you learn about yourself, the more flawed you feel, and the more you are separated from the part of yourself that is submerged.

You *identify* yourself as this flaw, this separation. As you grow, you gather evidence to substantiate your increasing sense of self-loathing. Defined by the dictates of the outside world, you develop life-shaping, life-warping rules that guide your growing up.

As you lose track of your Genuine Self, an Impostor emerges. This Impostor wears your clothes and answers to your name. The Impostor feels flawed. The Impostor begins to develop a personal drama that mirrors the drama around you and reflects the things you've learned and been told about yourself. Your behavior will begin to follow the warping rules that you have learned. In order to get along in the world that has made those rules, you, or rather your Impostor, will develop survival behavior. The Impostor will use survival techniques to get you from your childhood drama to adulthood, where you expect things to be different.

Once you're an adult, things aren't really so different. The Impostor has learned to *survive,* so you keep doing the same things and feeling the same way. You follow the warping rules of childhood. Because you haven't mastered your relationship to the past, you repeat it. You may have had long periods in which you seemed to have gotten in touch with your spirituality and your self-worth, coasting on a cloud of contentment, and then lost it all—returning to survival and old, familiar feelings.

Let's say you know you grew up in a (perhaps inadvertently) abusive family and a (definitely) abusive society. Let's say that as an adult you have recognized your unhappiness and have been told how to give up your codependence, leave substance abuse behind, and reclaim your inner child. Let's say you have even been shown the way to physical health. Let's say you've gotten magical answers from some magical person. Let's say you've successfully adhered to some pat happiness system.

Then why are you still not where you long to be? Why, though you may get a temporary reprieve, do you always seem to have to go back to square one whenever a new issue comes up in your life? Why is your recovery only skin-deep? Why does it seem that just when you are floating on a sea of well-being, with everything you desire in sight, something, in some area of your life, comes up to create a storm? A storm you've weathered before. Given what you know about yourself and how much help is available, why do you always seem to return to some version of the abusive, warping drama that you grew up with?

I think the answer is that you're addicted to it. *Your real issue is an addiction to your childhood drama.* You are addicted to the way your life has always been and you are addicted to the way you have always felt about yourself. So, when you seek help, you most likely choose dysfunctional recovery. *You are trapped in an addictive cycle that always brings you back to the pain and drama of childhood.* You have been treating the symptoms without having a clue what the disease is. You can't help it, for without an awareness of this very basic addiction, you have probably done the best that you could. You have become addicted to the sense of your flawed self. The addictions that you go to treat are actually activators of this deeper addiction to the way it has always been.

Here is what I mean. I was a cocaine addict. I did cocaine to feel better, feel smarter, be more creative, and to like myself. Or did I? I drank to feel better, too. I drank to avoid feeling socially retarded and to relax. I drank so that I could enjoy myself. Or did I? I became a profoundly effective teacher so that I could feel good about myself. I helped people so that they would love and revere me; this made me really know I was worthy of love. Or did it?

In retrospect I think that I did all of those things so that when the euphoria, the sense of well-being, or the high wore off, I could dip right back into my shame and self-loathing. I even remember, as a dieter, feeling some perverse relief in the shame I would feel when after a binge, I would get on the scale and have to face a ten-pound weight gain. I thought I wanted to be thin. Rather than the high, I was addicted to the crash.

What I was actually addicted to were the patterns that I learned as a child in a well-meaning, yet malfunctioning, family and social system. I was addicted to the drama and lack of self-worth that I grew up with. I was addicted to not being enough, to my fear, to my personal drama, and to the separation between who I really am, my Genuine Self, and who I believed myself to be, the Impostor. For this reason there was just so much well-being that I could handle, just so much success and love that could be tolerated before I'd need a fix of the old drama! Sound familiar?

Thus my substance abuse and compulsive behaviors were, in recovery jargon, the "enablers" of my addiction. I needed to touch my self-loathing. A failed romance or drugs would get me there. My cocaine habit enabled, or activated, my deeper habit of self-loathing and a life of drama. A hangover would remind me of the horrible, shameful person I really was.

I am not alone in this addiction.

A client whom I'll call Anne lived with a violent man. She had been beaten on many occasions. Whenever she was about to leave him, he became loving and sweet. She had always thought that she loved this "part" of him and that was why she stood by her man. But these grace periods never lasted too long. Something would trigger a new violent episode. It was Anne's impression that it was the spaces between the abuse that drew her to this man. She thought that the high she felt when he was good to her, and which represented love, was why she stayed. But what she discovered later was that only when she was feeling the shame and abuse of the beatings and violence did she know who she was. Then she was the worthless, frightened, hopeless child that the abuse of her youth had told her she was. Only then was she safe in the familiar sense of self-loathing and humiliation that she had grown up with. She was hooked on it.

Think about it a minute. How does this apply to your own life? It may be that your childhood was not as overtly abusive as Anne's, but look into your own history and see if this might not be true. What might you master if you could disengage from your core addiction to self-loathing?

If you can recognize that your core addiction still warps you, it would explain why much of the healing and recovery techniques that you pursue will have activated your personal and recurring drama. Many people who enter a crash course to self-love, recovery, and a new life find that they succumb to new versions of the old dysfunctions or malfunctions. And I believe that most of the systems that are designed to make you feel better about yourself and your life—all the way from psychoanalysis to New Age—carry within them the means to perpetuate themselves while leaving you still separated from your Genuine Self.

As you search for self-worth and salvation, you will be looking for parent replacements to "make better" the dysfunction your original family laid on you. This time, however, you turn your power over, not to Mama and Papa, but to lovers, gurus, self-proclaimed spokespersons for God or the Goddess, governments, therapists, and spiritual disciplines. *Someone* will save you, surely a real "grown-up" will appear to show you the way! While you live in the illusion that you are on the next path, you choose teachers and teachings that will ultimately lead you back to your cycle of basic addiction.

Can you not see that turning over your power to other people means a continued loss of self? Probably not. When you are caught in an addictive cycle, you can't perceive how you keep repeating malfunctional patterns. Once you have given your personal power away to some rigid belief system or some hip or not-so-hip pundit, you have repeated a childhood pattern that will ultimately keep your Genuine Self submerged in the drama you're seeking to escape.

False prophets—from TV evangelists to New Age ministers—will want to tell you how to be, what to think, and what's appropriate to feel. They will want you to do as they say (usually not as they do in their own lives) so that they can perpetuate the system that makes them right. From Pat Robertson to Marianne Williamson, there are those who will preach dogma from a book (in Robertson's case, the Bible; for Williamson, *A Course in Miracles*) and tell you that they have the inside track on what God wants. They assume that you don't have the brains and spirituality to come to your own sense of the words and to your own relationship with a spiritual source.

When you surrender your personal power to a system of belief, as you did in childhood, you are at the mercy of input from the world around you. Unlike what happened in childhood, this time you've chosen to give your power away. Your Impostor makes this choice because it is only safe when you are participating in a malfunctional, warped system. This choice is the Impostor's protection. It lets you think you are healthy when all you've done is trade systems. This way, when you can't be good enough for the new system, when the high wears off, you will be returned to your fix of the self-loathing drama that has you repeating your dysfunctional patterns.

If you get too close to breaking your patterns, your Impostor will try something to pull you back to your separation from your Genuine Self—certain people or events that will bring back the old familiar feelings and drama.

The dysfunction of the family is reflected all through society.

Government, politics, nationalism, education, and medicine, to name a few, are all based in rigid systems that perpetuate themselves rather than serve the well-being of society. Society, like the family, is caught in this addictive cycle of self-perpetuating denial and separation from the possibility of real growth and change.

Life Mastery is about breaking that cycle of separation and getting you back to your Genuine Self. *Life Mastery* differs from other recovery books and methods that you have pursued because it recognizes your core addiction to your childhood drama and this separation that you feel as a result. Unlike the guru/star-generated books you've read, it presents no system or dogma for you to follow. Rather, it guides you to discover your own healing path. To think for yourself. Unlike many other systems, Life Mastery does not require that you follow any rules or deny any reality. No tricks! It does not ask you to give your personal power away to anyone or to deny your instincts in favor of a set of pat answers or platitudes.

In fact, I am more interested in asking you questions than in giving you answers. You already know what you need, you just forgot. This book offers a journey out of forgetfulness toward self-Mastery.

Mastery implies that you live in reality and that acceptance of that reality leads you to your creativity, self-expression, and power. Mastery does not mean control; it means living in harmony with the many facets of your Genuine Self and recognizing the Genuine Self in others. It means living in the present, with your drama and history behind you, where they belong. It means lifting the veil of amnesia that has kept you from remembering that you are intrinsically loving, powerful, and worthy, though you may have been giving lip-service to the notion.

Deepak Chopra, author of *Quantum Healing* and *Perfect Health,* is a cutting-edge physician and practitioner of Ayurvedic medicine. He says that our worldview is created by our interpretation of our sensory experiences as we grow up. When these sensory experiences separate us from our Genuine Selves it takes a major shift in our perceptions and interpretations of past and present reality to effect a deep and lasting shift in our perception of ourselves. Our early sensory experience becomes imprinted on a cellular level. It is this experience that forms our core addiction.

Mastery will allow you to replace your core addiction with a strong sense of self. You will begin to master your relationship to your emotions, your body, your needs, your spiritual source, and to other people. You will be able to tap into a personal vision and one for the world in which you live. Once you can face your personal drama as something you are addicted to, exposing it and all of its activators to the light of truth, you can release it and experience an actual shift in your perspective of yourself. This shift is so profound that you actually are touched and moved by who you are. And you will experience your real self so intensely that you could not experience yourself as "the way you were" anymore. This means that the change is physiological. You can remember how it was, but you can't go back.

The process of Mastery is emotional, intellectual, physical, and spiritual all at once. It is *cellular.* Have you ever seen one of those cards that is filled with colored dots and asks you to "Find the flower"? You look and look, and for a while all you see are dots. Then suddenly your perception shifts, and there it is! A flower made of dots. The flower is there! Not only is it there, but you can no longer see this picture of a flower as a card full of dots. This perceptual shift is physiological. You know on a deep, visceral level that there is a flower, and so it won't go away or be forgotten. You can put the card in a drawer and forget about it for a year or so. If you clean the drawer and run across it, what you will discover is a card with a picture of a flower on it.

The truth permeates the illusion. Once you discover who you are on a level so deep that it shifts your perception from the picture your story has painted to the genuine picture, you will never again be able to perceive yourself as unlovable or undeserving. The addiction to your drama will be replaced by freedom, power, and creativity. Your personal story will no longer hold you.

I know it may be very frightening to think of giving up the core addiction that has come to be your identity. It feels life-threatening to break the rules and malfunctioning patterns that you've lived by since childhood. Think about this: if it's frightening to you, can you imagine how threatened the addiction feels? Imagine how your Impostor feels. In order to stay alive your Impostor keeps you in denial and illusions. If you let go of your drama, your Impostor no longer exists. Its life depends on your addiction. It wants you to think that *your* life depends on it. This will become clear as we travel the road to Mastery.

Each of you will experience mastery personally, in your own way.

Each in your own way can pierce through the amnesia that keeps you from knowing and expressing your Genuine Self. As you allow yourself to feel safe and surrender to the process, that Genuine Self will emerge to live fully, functionally, wholly. In all of the years that I have worked with others, first in the theater and entertainment industry and for the better part of the last decade in the AIDS/HIV community, it is the Genuine Self has been the elusive object of desire. Until I understood my own addictive relationship to my personal drama, that self always appeared to be close, but just out of reach. I would even touch it for a moment now and then, before it would slip from my grasp.

AIDS put a different light on everything. The urgency that is present for those confronting mortality on a daily basis brought all of this into clear focus. When the search for self is accelerated by the threat of physical extinction, things that have been fuzzy sharpen up. AIDS has made one thing clear. You can have your drama or you can have your life. While this book is not about AIDS/HIV, it is a through line that has expedited my quest. AIDS is a microcosm of the planet and its issues. AIDS is an immune dysfunction. The mechanism within the body that protects it from infection is broken down in the way the environment is breaking down. The ozone layer is the immune system of the planet. There are holes in the ozone layer.

AIDS reflects the same dysfunction and lack of consciousness that permeates every aspect of society. The systems that surround the AIDS crisis are a reflection of dysfunctional family systems. The way AIDS has been dealt with in the world is a mirror of the lack of consciousness that has allowed pollution, the depletion of natural resources, wars, famine, prejudice, greed, and other things that separate mankind from its potential.

AIDS has brought great clarity for me to the issues of life on both a personal and societal basis. I offer that clarity to you in the words of people whom I have worked with over the years in a heightened reality that eventually brought light for me to an ancient truth.

That truth was profoundly stated long ago by Swami Muktenanda, my first and only guru to date. He said, "Enlightenment begins the moment one recognizes oneself." This means that you already are the person you seek to become. Your actions may reflect your drama and be played out by your Impostor, but your Genuine Self is there. All you have to do is to recognize who you are and have always been. Less profoundly stated: you're all right already. You knew that once, when you were very small; but all of the input of your history, and your perception of that history has given you a kind of amnesia. You've forgotten who you really are, but you can awaken from the amnesia your core addiction causes as if it has been a drugged stupor, and remember who you are. To remember requires seeing and experiencing beyond the drama, beyond the separation you have felt for too long. To remember is to be whole. To remember is the first part of Mastery.

How to Use
Life Mastery

I've been a meditator and a meditation teacher for a long
time, so it was hard for me to switch techniques until I
realized I wasn't switching. I was trying something new.

Chuck Baier, *New York, 1986*

IN USING THE PROCESS OF LIFE MASTERY THERE ARE MANY HELPFUL TOOLS
AND SIMPLE TECHNIQUES THAT WILL AID YOU ALONG YOUR WAY. You are the
best resource that you have for moving forward in your life and filling
it with nurturing, loving experiences and people. You'll find a series of
exercises throughout this book. Some of them will ask you to write
things down, to make lists, or otherwise to keep in touch with feelings
and needs. Other exercises take the form of visualizations or guided
meditations. With regard to all of the exercises it is important to keep
in mind that they are tools for the discovery of the basic truths you may
have forgotten in the growing up and separation process, and for the
release of your attachment to the past, to mere survival, to the patterns
that keep your childhood drama a present-day reality.

These exercises are not intended to become a burden or a way of
life. They are here to support your Mastery, not to become one more
thing to have to deal with. Some exercises will be appropriate for you
and germane to your issues, while others may not. But be sure that
when you choose the ones that attract you, you do not mistake disinter-
est and irrelevance for resistance and discomfort. I do suggest that if
you feel real resistance to doing something that you try it. Your
resistance might be the Impostor keeping you from something that
could shift your experience. If it is your genuine natural instinct that
says, "I don't need this one," then follow that instinct. You can always
come back to it.

You may find yourself skipping around the book to the issues that seem most pressing. Even so, I suggest that you begin with the first visualization. It sets the stage.

There is no right or wrong way to go about the process of Life Mastery. There are plenty of disciplines and techniques out there that are as rigid as the systems that you grew up with, but in *Life Mastery* I want to provide you with the guidance and structure you need to define your own goals, gain your own experience, and have a profoundly good time.

About the Visualizations

The visualizations will take you on a journey designed to allow you to look at certain areas of your life. Once you are in them, if the path your unconscious presents to you differs from what the visualization encourages, stay on your own path. Your unconscious knows better what you need to look at than the visualization does. In other words, if the visualization says, "See yourself at six" and you see yourself yesterday, stick with yesterday.

The visualizations are written out for you. You may want to record the words of these processes on tape in your own voice, since you might benefit from the reinforcement of being your own guide. You may also read them aloud or silently to yourself, and allow your response to flow either by pausing to close your eyes or by staying with the words on the page. Remember, however you do this is just fine. There is no specific way to sit, no special breathing other than deeply, no special room setup or music. *You* get to set the stage and design the set. You can create and discover the way that will work best for you.

These exercises are used to bring to the surface what already lies in your unconscious, and to release the self-love and truth you already possess. Don't worry if it takes you a while to grow absorbed in a visualization. If you are not a very visual person you may bring up memories and sensations in other ways. Allow yourself the time to discover your own way.

You may already meditate or do guided imagery of some kind. If you already have a shrine or special place use it; if not you can find an area that feels safe and comfortable. Try to give yourself plenty of time to do these visualizations and to assimilate their information and feelings. Glance through them before you begin so that you have some idea of the impact that they will have. Remember, your well-being is the point of doing all of this. It is best not to jar yourself out of an experience before you are ready or be interrupted by the telephone.

You may like the lights dim and music playing. You may feel more comfortable in full lotus on the floor or relaxed but alert on the couch. There's a big difference between a visualization and a nap! You may like music. You may like quiet. You may like candlelight. The point is to create a nurturing and safe place for yourself.

Many of you who do guided imagery have a technique for getting into the process that has worked for you. Please feel free to use it. The best state for the visualizations that follow is a relaxed body and alert unconscious. For this reason, the entry technique I prefer uses energy to raise the natural vibration rate within your body. It is also a technique I use when I am exhausted and don't have time to lie down. The idea is to picture drawing energy from the earth and from the universe. There is plenty out there. Why not tap into it and energize yourself? As you do the visualizations take all the time you need. Be generous with yourself. The most crucial places to give yourself time will be marked . . . just as a reminder.

> *Close your eyes for a moment, even if you will be reading the*
>   *visualization.*
> *Breathe deeply through your body.*
> *Just feel your breath coming in and out of your body.*
> *Sense the rhythm of it.*
> *See where you are holding tension.*
> *Send your breath to these areas of tension to soothe them and re-*
>   *lax them, as if your breath could massage the tension away.*
> *Imagine the tension leaving your body with each exhalation.*
> *Take all the time you need . . .*
> *Feel the breath flowing in and out of your body.*
> *Breathe very deeply and hold that breath for a moment.*
> *When you exhale let out as loud a sound as you can.*
> *Take another very deep breath.*
> *With your next breath, imagine that you bring into your body*
>   *energy from the center of the earth.*

A great stream of energy from the center of the earth.
This earth upon which we live, where we grow and are nourished.
This earth, with its constant cycles and changes.
Feel the vibration of the energy from the earth through your whole
  body.
Feel that vibration.
Let it vibrate in harmony with your own energy.
Send the vibration to any places in your body where you still feel
  tension.
Let the vibration rise.
As you inhale bring in more energy.
As you exhale allow yourself to release tension.
Let your body relax.
With your next breath imagine a flood of energy
  from the infinite universe flowing into your body.
There is a vast and endless source of energy there.
Feel its vibration.
It has a powerful vibration.
The vibration of infinity.
Feel it vibrate in harmony with the energy from the center of the
  earth and your own energies.
Let the vibration rise.
Let it awaken your consciousness and open your heart.
Let the energy vibrate around your heart center.
Feel the expansion.

Imagine now that all of that energy begins to turn to light.
As it turns to light let it radiate from your heart center
  through your body and beyond.
Let it radiate beyond you until it fills your field of vision
  and becomes a place in which to discover what you will learn
  in the visualization.

This is the place where the images that your unconscious
and your imagination offer you will be available to you.

I'll include this section with the first visualization in the book, which should allow you to grow familiar with it. Now you are ready to do whatever visualization is called for. You are energized and relaxed and have a clear space in which to create and experience.

About Breathing

In the visualizations and other exercises I will often remind you to breathe deeply. You are much more open and in touch with your feelings when you breathe deeply. I have found that most people breathe just about enough to keep their blood and brain oxygenated and that's it. In a world where feelings are suppressed or too uncomfortable we've become shallow breathers. Try it. Take a few deep breaths. Not too fast, though, you don't want to hyperventilate. Just breathe deeply through your body and see how you feel.

Often, in visualizations and other exercises, you will be asked to breathe deeply and see how you feel about yourself. As you develop new skills for leaving past feelings and behavior patterns behind, it may be necessary to breathe deeply and make a reality check or give yourself a moment or two to see what is actually happening in the present moment. All of this will become clear as we proceed.

About Sound

In many of the visualizations and emotional exercises you will be given time to let out a sound. I would suggest that you go for it. Don't worry about the neighbors! You may have to find a really safe place or warn others that you may feel like crying or shouting and that you are all right. There is a lifetime of suppressed history and feeling trapped inside your body. It is time to release it. It will really allow you to feel fabulous!

Writing Things Down

In the same way that sound releases feelings and history from your body, writing down your feelings helps to clear your mind and provide another venue for your feelings and thoughts. Once you put pen to paper, you can begin to see the patterns of your life and get a different experience of the way you operate. It can be very valuable to go back and see where you've been, where you are, what's really going on. You can pour your heart out.

What you write doesn't have to be real, responsible, well-written, or even what you really mean. Your journal is a place for "dumping." Here you can blame someone for something, even if you know better. You can whine. You can dump your feelings, air your grievances, spill your guts. It might help to write on loose paper so that you can read it over and over until you no longer need to see the words. You may want to burn some of what you write. It's a nice ritual.

A journal is a powerful tool. Your journal can be used to write down your dreams, thoughts, and feelings (other than dumping, and maybe some of that, too) and to do the exercises that need to be written. It is an ideal place to record the discoveries, questions, memories, and feelings that come up during the visualizations. It will be a remarkable document of your journey to Mastery.

Mastering the Past

Mastering the Past

It's like someone gave me an injection of self-doubt when I was real small and it's taken years and years of trial and error until I got it out of my system. System is the operative word here, 'cause I'd set my life up in the same system that brought me the doubt so there was no way to feel secure.

Robert Santoro, *New York, 1989*

MASTERING THE PAST IS THE FIRST STEP IN THE PROCESS OF LIFE MASTERY. Until you are able to allow your past to become just that, history, you will be run by it. In the section that follows I will explore the sources of the malfunction that plagues and distorts out adult lives. Many of you have been delving into your past in a way that actually keeps you attached to it, serving your addiction to your childhood drama. That is counterproductive; that makes your exploration an activator of your addictions. What we want to do in these pages is to deactivate, disengage, let you leave the dramas of your past behind.

The first step in deactivating the past is to discover the origins of your sense of self and your attitudes toward the world around you that were given to you as you grew up. The visualization I will offer you in this section will put you in touch with these sources. Once you've completed the visualization, you will begin to see how the rules that guided your growing up within the family and societal systems that surrounded you were created, and how these rules distorted your Genuine Self. You will look at the behavior you adapted to survive your childhood and how firmly entrenched in that behavior you have become. You will also begin to discover the difference between that behavior and who you really are. This becomes difficult because as we grow up we are rewarded or punished based on our behavior.

I did a workshop in New York called "Are the Words *Dysfunctional* and *Family* Redundant?" The phrase *dysfunctional family* has become such a catchall and cliché that we hardly stop anymore to see what it really means to us as individuals. Let's take as a basic assumption that most of us come from dysfunctional family and social systems.

For better or worse, for richer or poorer, your childhood shaped the adult that you are today. Even if you were lucky enough to have grown up in a healthy atmosphere and felt the love of your parents, the systems outside the family, such as school, peers, church (or synagogue, mosque, what have you) can separate you from your Genuine Self. If you did not experience nurturing and safety as you grew up, if you have not learned self-love, then you have grown up experiencing yourself as other than your true self. Your relationship to your family and the systems that surrounded you determine your sense of yourself and the world. Those relationships form the basis of your personal belief systems—what you believe about yourself and how the world is.

What is a system? Among Webster's many definitions of the word, several seem to be the most relevant to our exploration. Slightly paraphrased, they are: an assemblage of parts forming a whole; due method or orderly manner of arrangement or procedure. Another is: the structure or organization of society, business, or politics, or of society in general. And another: a number of heavenly bodies or other aspects of life associated and acting together *according to natural laws.*

Healthy, natural systems create order and allow society to function. The key to a healthy system is that it operate *according to natural law.* In a healthy system, nature is honored and the natural spirit and needs of humans are met. In a system that supports nature, a child is allowed to grow up with security and freedom of expression and creativity. A child has a natural knowing and is very attuned to the flow of life.

In nature, systems are fluid and growing. Variety, spontaneity, and expansion are the hallmark of nature. The Solar System is orderly and yet always in flux, always changing, always surprising. One season follows another in natural order, and yet each winter and each spring bring with them completely different aspects of nature. Nature's systems encourage growth and survival by virtue of their adaptability.

Human systems often become rigid and stifling. They strangle creativity and suppress uniqueness. Human beings create systems to understand and to manage what cannot be explained, or to control whatever threatens the system. We do it to ourselves and we do it to nature. Look at man's relationship to nature. We "harness it," "control it," "make it serve us," and all without noticing that we are depleting and destroying our natural resources. *What we do to nature we do to ourselves.*

In order to perpetuate the human social system and override nature, we have embraced greed, self-interest, and righteousness. We have created guilt, self-loathing, and resentment. We have tried to invalidate uniqueness and spontaneity. While creativity sustains nature's systems, it becomes a threat to ours. Malfunctioning systems are closed systems and have no room for spontaneity and change.

When you were a child and expressed anything that threatened the status quo, you were taught to conform. Because your Genuine Self was warped by a stifling system, you've become trapped in your addiction to your drama and an unnatural closed system about who you are. This is where we will begin the work of exploring the systems that have held you prisoner and releasing their hold on you. As you shed the systems of your past you will begin the journey to Mastery.

The Roots of Drama Lie in Childhood

I spent a lot of time as an artist and a meditator finding my way out of the systems that I had been expected to conform to. Even when I was a little boy, I felt like a warrior fighting, to be able to do life my way.

Victor Phillips, *New York, 1987*

WHEN YOU WERE BORN, YOU WERE ALIVE WITH POSSIBILITIES AND LOVE. Outside of bodily functions, you did two things very well, things that came just as naturally: you felt, and you expressed. One of the first things that the system imposed on you was limitation to your self-expression. As soon as your crying became uncomfortable for the adult world, you were trained to be appropriate, to suppress your tears.

Perhaps you had a pacifier stuffed in your mouth. A pacifier is not a response to a natural need. Quite literally, you were stifled. What's a little kid to do? You suppress your cries to survive. You suppress your natural instincts in order to make sense of the adult world. You suppress in order not to shake the very foundation of your world. You suppress in order to honor your father and mother and the way it has always been.

As you grew up you actually may have been told, or sensed from what was expressed around you, what was okay and what was not okay to express. Perhaps it was not all right to be afraid. Perhaps it was not all right to be angry with your parents. Perhaps it was not all right to speak your truth if it deviated from the family line. Perhaps you grew up to be well schooled in denial and some family secrets; after a while you may not even have dared to tell *yourself* the truth. You may not now be free to express or explore anything that creates discomfort or threatens the way things have always worked in your family or in your life.

Sure, as a kid you needed to be socialized. You needed to understand that your actions have repercussions in the lives and world around you. You needed to learn what is dangerous and what is not. Children need to be told if there is a clear and present danger. Traffic is dangerous. Drinking Drāno can kill you. Slapping your brother will hurt your brother and probably get you hurt in return.

Children need to have healthy limits set for them. They intuitively know a lot, but they do have much to learn from the adult world. Some of what adults teach is powerful and pertinent. These good things do allow children to develop within healthy guidelines *but do not dictate the limits* of their experience of self or the world. Socialization can be freeing when it serves the well-being of the child rather than the well-being of the system. It can offer a child a framework in which to grow and discover. But too often, malfunction and abuse are offered in the name of socialization. It suppresses uniqueness, creativity, natural responses, and the Genuine Self.

It doesn't take physical or sexual abuse for you to define your childhood as malfunctioning. Abuse comes in all shapes and sizes and from many quarters. So whether you know it or not, you have been abused. Mom and Dad are not the only abusers. Abuse comes from peers, from teachers, from extended family, from television, society, and the systems within which they exist.

From religious schools to family tyranny, you are all familiar with the more dramatic ways our systems and unnatural rules have warped you and abused you. In my workshops I hear an endless litany of the painful ways in which participants were brutalized and hurt as children. All kinds of abuse will submerge your Genuine Self into your unconscious. The abuse and inhumanity that you may have suffered most likely occurred with deadly and relative silence. It may have been blatant or it may have been so subtle that it went unnoticed, such as inferences about a child's physical beauty or expectations of achievement. It may have been the result of well-meaning efforts, discipline, or misplaced kindness, such as helping a child when the help makes her feel stupid. No matter how ordinary your upbringing was, you existed and continue to exist in a world that has lost its natural path.

Abuse runs the gamut from incest to the subtle undermining of a child's self-esteem. Incest can be so damaging that the memory of it is submerged until well into adulthood—and yet it informs every relationship and interpersonal reaction in the life of the victim. The subtle end of the spectrum can be almost as damaging, even simple things, such as constant teasing, always being compared to someone else, being forced to eat food that you don't like, and always being given arbitrary ultimatums and "because I said so" 's.

It is abusive for a child to have to grow up too soon, to be the family caregiver. It is abusive for a child to raise siblings or to tend an alcoholic parent. It is abusive to force a child to see the world exactly as adults do. It is abusive to disavow a child's feelings and perceptions. It is abusive to coerce and manipulate with guilt or threaten a child with God's wrath. It is abusive to teach a child to suppress natural emotions. It is abusive to humiliate a child in front of a class of peers. Severe discipline is abusive. It is abusive for an adult to hit a child or to explode all over him with pent-up or unresolved emotional issues. It is abusive for an adult to take a dysfunctional past out on anyone; it is not a child's responsibility to bear the brunt of any adult's unresolved past.

Perhaps even after all of these examples, you may not think of yourself as abused. You may not consider your parents abusers. Surely abusers never consider themselves as such. Many abusers are well-meaning parents who love their children. Many abusers are so victimized by their own pasts that all they can do is act out in the present. Many abusers are parents or teachers or clergy who are doing what they think is best. They do it for your own good. They do it because that's the way their parents or mentors did it. Because that's what the system told them to do.

I remember when my baby sister was born. After I'd waited for months for my new playmate, this little bundle was brought home. Was I supposed to play with this squealing blanket? My parents, trying to make it all right, informed me that I loved her. Lots of parents do this. Inadvertently, they were abusive, because they replaced my reality with theirs. I wasn't so sure I loved her. It didn't feel like love. But because I was constantly assured that I did love her, and because I knew love was "nice" and "good," I said I did. The word *love* seemed like a mask for abandonment and resentment. I had no name for these feelings. While images of the new baby being thrown out with the trash or devoured by wild animals flashed through my mind, I smiled and suppressed my upset. I was told this was love. And to this day my reaction to love sometimes includes resentment and fear of abandonment. If I'm not careful, I can faithfully re-create what I was told as a child.

There is no area that more clearly demonstrates the struggle between natural instincts and the system than the limits imposed on children around sexuality. Children possess natural knowing and natural boundaries; once they have some degree of socialization and some basic skills they can do quite well. If they eat strawberries, they will feel good. If they eat poison berries, they will throw up. Chances are they'll steer clear of the poison berries. If they put their little fingers in a flame, they will quickly draw them away in pain. They'll get the lesson. Kids are pretty smart that way. There are other things that nature cannot point to but adults can. Children still need guidance and limits; they also need protection from actual hazards such as window ledges or firearms.

Now try to imagine yourself as a small child. You have no lascivious or lecherous impulses. You just have curiosity and natural instincts, right? You explore or touch everything. If you don't break something valuable, grown-ups usually applaud your exploration. You touch your hair. You say "hair." Terrific! New word. Then you, still the same sweet child, touch your genitals! It seems natural! No flame, no poison. No clear and present danger.

Unless an adult is clear and present. Then all hell breaks loose. Normally composed, competent adults go berserk! They swoop down into your childish natural space and tell you it's not okay! They invade personal, sexual, and intellectual space to get their own point across and set their own limits for the child. They invade the child's boundaries and impose their own fear. "Don't do that!" But why not? "Wait till your father gets home!" Uh-oh! "Don't you ever let me see you do that again!"

So you don't! They never see you do it again. This doesn't necessarily mean that you never do it again. You may go underground, do it in secret. You can't understand what's wrong. You only know you must have done something very wrong and in fact that you yourself *are* wrong. You get confused and scared. If you weren't supposed to do it, why would it feel so good?

The same goes for touching the genitals of another child. Getting caught at that puts you into a new category. Pervert! Wouldn't it make sense to deal with sex the way other aspects of growing up are dealt with? But most grown-ups haven't dealt with their own sexuality. They grew up in a system that limited their ability to cope. Their parents handled it the same way, so they pass the malfunction right along!

We have to learn to suppress what comes naturally and live within the system to survive. *In order to make sense of the adult world into which we are going to grow up, we must make our very own instincts and self wrong.* I actually do mean "make ourselves wrong." As children we don't have the information to see that the system doesn't work, or that we have broken the rules of the system, and that is why we are in trouble. We just think we are bad. We are sacrificed to the system, and we begin to replace our reality with that of the system. *The* system becomes our system.

And from this warped system comes our sense of ourselves. As we give ourselves away to the system, we begin to separate from our Genuine Selves. The system teaches us our sense of self and the world around us. Who we think we are is determined by the input of the outside world. The input that represents the system and disavows our nature drives a wedge in our relationship with ourselves.

The following is an exercise that I do in many workshops. It is a visualization that guides you to the events, people, and moments that contribute to your separation from who you really are. As the separation unfolds, the Impostor takes over the identity of your Genuine Self. You can also use this visualization to see how the same events and people set up a lot of rules for you to live by. To begin to repair the damage and gain some Mastery over the past, it is necessary to go directly to these sources.

In the visualization you'll be asked to imagine an endless corridor. Both sides of the expanse will be lined with doors. Behind each door is an event or person or time that contributed to forming some unsupportive aspect of your sense of self and created a rule to live by.

It is essential that as you do this work you keep breathing deeply through your body, because it's impossible to be in touch with your feelings unless energy is flowing. Breath is a connection to your feelings.

You will be asked to choose a door, and as you go through it, you will find yourself immersed in an experience from childhood that gave you a sense of yourself and the world.

Once you're in that space, let yourself take plenty of time to really observe the incident. Then breathe through your body and see how you felt about yourself. You'll be asked who was there and what was happening. Stay in touch with the feelings as you allow the event to unfold and see the rules that resulted about yourself and the world around you. What did you decide and cast in stone?

When you've discovered what you needed to, you'll be asked to move on. This is how you will begin to get a sense of what your personalized belief system is. This "Corridor Visualization" will set the stage for much of what is to follow, but remember, if it takes a while to get into it, that's fine. This process is quite long, so get yourself comfortable in a secure and safe place. Put music on if you wish. I will repeat the relaxation process that you read earlier this first time through, but use your own if you prefer.

Close your eyes for a moment.
Breathe deeply through your body.
Just feel your breath coming in and out of your body.
Sense the rhythm of it.
See where you are holding tension.
Feel the breath flowing in and out of your body.
Breathe very deeply and hold that breath for a moment.
When you exhale let out as loud a sound as you can.
Take another very deep breath.

With your next breath, imagine that you bring into your body energy from the center of the earth.
This earth upon which we live, where we grow and are nourished.
This earth, with its constant cycles and changes.
Feel the vibration of the energy from the center of the earth through your whole body.
Feel that vibration and let it vibrate in harmony with your own energy.
Send the vibration to any places in your body where you feel tension.

Let the vibration rise.
As you inhale bring in more energy.
As you exhale allow yourself to release tension.

With your next breath imagine a flood of energy from the infinite
universe flowing into your body.
Feel its vibration.
It has a powerful vibration.
The vibration of infinity.
Feel it vibrate in harmony with the energy from the center of the
earth and your own energies.
Let the vibration rise.
Let it awaken your consciousness and open your heart.
Feel the expansion.
Imagine now that all of that energy begins to turn to light.
As it turns to light let it fill your field of vision
and become a place in which to discover what you will learn
in the visualization.

In the light become aware of a very long corridor.
It is very long.
You can't see the end.
Doors line the length of the corridor on both sides.
They are closed.
Behind each of these doors is a time or a person or an event
that shaped your sense of yourself.
Behind each door is an experience that helped you decide
who you are and reinforced that belief.
There are many such experiences.

Go up to one of the doors.
Breathe through your body.

Be aware of how you feel as you stand there . . .

Put your hand on the handle.

*Take a deep breath, open the door, and go into the space that
    lets you see a time when you began to create your sense of your-
    self . . .*

Who is there?

Is anyone there?

Where are you?

Let out a sound.

*Let out a sound that will release and express the feelings
    that are going on in your body.*

Sound is a brilliant release.

How do you feel about yourself?

What is happening or being said?

*What did you decide about who you are or how life is going
    to be?*

What began in this instant?

What was happening?

How did it feel to be you?

What did you believe about yourself?

Let yourself feel the experience in your body.

How did it feel?

Let yourself be right there.

What did you make up in that moment?

How did this help to set up your personal drama?

Let yourself discover the answer.

Here is part of the drama that you relive.

Let it come from your feelings rather than the mind.

From your natural knowing rather than thoughts.

What does it feel like?

*When you know all you need to know for right now, turn and face
    the door. Get ready to leave this space.*

As you do, close the door behind you and let it all go.
Let out a sound.
Breathe deeply and just be there with your feelings.
Move to another door.

(Repeat this as many more times as feels right for you, always
remembering to breathe deeply, let out sound, and let yourself have
whatever feelings appear. Then:)

Turn and look down the corridor.
See that all of the remaining doors that line its walls are ajar.
Behind each of these doors is a time or a person
     or an experience that added to your sense of yourself.
Begin to go down the corridor.
Pause before each door and look into the space.
See what is there, breathe through your body
     and see how it affected your body.

Enter every door until all of the doors close behind you.
Move toward the light.
Look into the light.
As you do be aware that what you are seeing is your own
     reflection.
The light is a true reflection of who you are.
Spirit, energy, that sense of yourself that sleeps within the energy
     that now vibrates with brilliance within your body.
For a moment recognize yourself.

See your true reflection.
This is who you are.
Light, energy, love.

What lies behind the doors is a reflection of history
*   and experiences and interpretation and judgment.*
You are perfectly reflected in the light.
And in that light make a commitment to your own well-being.
Make a commitment to let go of that in your life which does not
*   nurture you and to embrace that which does.*
Make a commitment to the quality of your life.

Begin to allow your breathing to return to normal.
Allow your awareness to return to your surroundings:
*   the sounds in the room, the temperature,*
*   your body as it relates to the space around you.*
Take time to acclimate yourself, and when you are ready, open
*   your eyes. Look around you.*
Just give yourself a few minutes to sit with what you've dis-
*   covered.*
You may want to write for a while.

The systems that we live within will have hold of us until we are willing to make the commitment to pull away from them and go forward. It is hard to make a commitment to move on unless you are committed to your own well-being. That commitment is the first real decisive step.

Commitment to Your Well-Being

I *couldn't believe how everything lined up for me once I was willing to make the commitment! I put out the word, and for once it was more than a word. I was willing to back up my word with action. Things started to fall into place and the next thing I knew I was actually getting what I wanted. It makes me wonder what I did with all of that energy before and it makes me sad that I waited so long.*

Steven Bradley, *Houston, 1988*

WITHOUT COMMITMENT TO YOUR OWN WELL-BEING, IT WILL BE VERY DIFFI-CULT TO BREAK OUT OF YOUR DRAMA AND CREATE THE LIFE THAT YOU WANT. If you are to repair the separation that the malfunction of your childhood has created and have a life of wonder, fulfillment, and happiness, you'll need an active, consistent willingness to change. Joseph Campbell said in *The Power of Myth* that "People say that what we are all seeking is a meaning for life. I don't think that's what we're really seeking. I think that what we're seeking is an experience of being alive, so that our life experiences on the purely physical plane will have resonance within our innermost being and reality, so that we feel the rapture of being alive. . . ." Commitment! Without it we are doomed to a life without rapture.

If you have spent the better part of your life beating yourself up, being abused, sabotaging yourself, and sacrificing your well-being to others, committing to your own well-being is a real stretch. But as soon as you make the commitment, you feel power. You've made a clear statement to yourself, to those around you, and to the universe that things are in for a change. The change that follows will amaze you.

First of all, you will be able to assess the events and circumstances of your life in terms of whether they serve or thwart your commitment to your well-being. Second, you will find yourself acting to support your commitment. Third, you will be impelled toward the things you need in order to honor that commitment.

If you want to know how this commitment business works, look at what constitutes your life overall. It will tell you what you are already committed to. You have most likely been unconsciously committed to your drama and to maintaining the system you've come to live by, however unhappily. How else could it stay so firmly in place? *It is your unconscious commitments that thwart your conscious efforts to commit to your well-being.*

What are you already unhealthily committed to? Say you have been trying to have a relationship that is open and honest and intimate and instead have withheld openness, honesty, and intimacy. Or you've had relationships with people who have trouble with intimacy. In either case, your commitment is to withholding, to keeping intimacy at bay. Once you recognize this, you can begin to see where the need to keep intimacy at bay comes from. When you are basically committed to your well-being, you can change your commitment from protecting your childhood fear of intimacy to having intimacy in your adult life.

If you have committed three hundred times to a diet and you always come short of your goal and put on not only the weight that you lost, but a few extra pounds, it is time to ask yourself where your commitment actually lies. Is it to being slimmer and healthier and liking the way you look, or is it to honoring a childhood commitment to not fitting in, not pleasing your parents, not being accepted?

Your commitments, deliberate or unconscious, have great effect in your life. When you become aware of these commitments, you have a choice whether to continue them. When you can replace your unsupportive commitments with commitments that align with your well-being, you will have freedom and power.

How do you begin the process of supportive commitment? Once, years ago, I was in Gestalt therapy. The therapist asked me to make a list of everything I would do for myself if I thought that I was worth it. I did that, and when I came back the next week with my list, she asked me to read it to her. Then she gave me an assignment. Begin to do the things on the list.

I want you to make a similar list. First I want you to do a little visualizing. You will take a journey through different aspects of your life to see if you are living it the way you want to. If not, what might you secretly be committed to that is in the way? Beyond that, what could you do to have what you want?

Find a comfortable place in a soothing, nurturing spot, where you can relax, but not enough to drift off. Begin by taking some very deep relaxing breaths and being very aware of your body and your feelings.

As you breathe deeply, begin to allow your field of vision to fill with light.
In that light begin to see your reflection.
Look into your eyes.
See how you feel about yourself . . .
Is this the way you want to feel?
Look deep within.
Begin to take a look at your life.

Physically, how do you present yourself?
Look at your reflection.
Take a deep breath and see how you feel about yourself.
Is it how you want to represent yourself?
Take your time.
See what comes up as you look . . .
Keep breathing deeply.
What would you change?
What keeps you from doing that?
What about your health and body?
If they do not make you sing with joy, how would you rather feel?
What would you change?
How would you rather feel?
Give yourself lots of time.
Keep looking.
How do you feel?

*What about your home and other personal environments
  where you spend time?*

*If they aren't the way you want them, given the reality of your life,
  how could you have them be more nurturing, more wonderful?*

What would you need to do?

What could they look like?

Take your time.

How do you feel?

What stands between you and having it be this way?

Have you made some commitment not to have what you want?

What could you do to change that?

What's going on in your body right now?

What about your job or other ways you spend your time?

Is it the way you want it?

If not, what could you do differently?

What would you rather be doing?

And what about other things you do?

How rich and fulfilling would you like these experiences to be?

What could keep you from being fulfilled and successful?

*Is there something that keeps you from going after what you
  want?*

What is it?

Have you somehow committed to limiting yourself?

What would you have to do to have it be the way you want?

How would you want your life to look?

Now take a moment to look at the quality of your relationships.

Are they the way you want them?

How would you rather have them be?

What would reflect the well-being that you deserve?

See how you feel about yourself in your relationships.

One by one, catch a glimpse of the people in your life.
Do they nurture and support you?
Do you tell the truth to each other?
Are these relationships offering you the quality that you really
*   want?*

In the relationships that do not nurture you,
*   can you see why you stay in them?*
Is there some unconscious commitment to not having rich,
*   rewarding relationships?*
Is there some commitment to not allowing the kind of intimacy
*   and nurturing that you deserve into your life?*
What would you need to do to have your relationships work?
What would you have to commit to?

Take your time.
Let these hidden commitments appear naturally . . .
You don't have to make sense of any of it.
No one is watching.
It's your movie.
When you've run the film to the end and feel a release,
*   get a pad or journal and a pen.*

Take out your journal and write down all of the things that you would have in your life if you thought you deserved them and there was no unhealthy commitment in the way. You may want to start with the things that you saw in your visualization, but don't limit yourself.

- What do you want to have in your life?
- What are the things that you want to do?
- What are the things that you want to stop doing or have happen?
- Whom do you want to be in a relationship with?

- How do you want to be treated?
- What do you want to change?
- What do you want your place in the world to be?

Just write without thought to how feasible any of it is, how possible, how probable. Just write. Make it wonderful and full and rich. Let your fantasies go.

When you have completed the list, go through it and check off the things that are within your power to create—the doables. These are the items that do not depend on anyone else or anything else. (There's a section on control issues coming up, but for our purposes, it's the difference between saying that you want an intimate, loving relationship and saying that you want an intimate, loving relationship with someone in particular. The first is expansive and possible, the second leaves your well-being in the hands of someone in particular, when right now you want to create the elements of your well-being in the realm of the possible. Get it? If not, just proceed as if you did. You'll get it later on!)

For the doables, write down the specific actions it would take to make them happen. (Some may be as simple as cleaning up your house and slapping a coat of white paint on the walls, or as difficult as telling someone that you don't like the way they treat you.) What you are doing is making a list of the things that would create well-being for you and the steps to making that happen.

Commitment is a powerful tool, but commitment backed up by action is a life force. Commitment and action are the recovery tools to break out of your system. Pick a few of the least threatening things on the list to start with. Begin by acting on these things as a demonstration of your commitment to your well-being.

As you continue through the processes and revelations that lie in store for you, the doing will become as second nature as the commitment. When this shift occurs, everything that you need to support your well-being will appear. It will be there as surely as everything you have needed to support your addiction to your drama has been there.

In my workshops I pass out a couplet by Goethe about commitment and action. It was sent to me as a New Year's card long ago, by a friend in New York, designer Chris Jones, and it sums up what

I've just been speaking about. It is about this kind of conscious commitment—a commitment that will bring with it the ingredients to attract your well-being.

> W*hatever you can do, or dream you can do, begin it.*
>
> *Boldness has genius and power and magic in it, begin it now!*
>
> Goethe

Through the visualization, the list you made, and the action you take, you are committing to doing and experiencing whatever it takes to break the hold the past has on you: to tell the truth, to let go of the things that no longer serve you, and to embrace those that do. In other words, you are committing to being *who you really are* and allowing your life to reflect that spirit. Commitment and action!

The Impostor Surviving the System

It always seemed to me that whatever I did I was in trouble. I was the bad kid in the family. It was almost as if I was cast in the roll of troublemaker, and in order to keep up my place in the scheme of things I had to keep being bad and causing trouble. Me mum, she'd smack me around and tell me I was no good. I've felt bad all of my life and now, as if to prove it I've got this bad thing [AIDS], and I give it to my kid. I am bad, I just am.

Anna Krimmer, *Glasgow, 1987*

CHILDHOOD CREATES A SEPARATION FROM WHO YOU REALLY ARE. You have become an Impostor. As you grew up your Genuine Self became confused, and soon you forgot who you really are. As a veil of amnesia enfolded you, the Impostor began to emerge to take your place. But the genuine you has not gone, it has just submerged, waiting to be rediscovered.

Before conception, you are energy. As the shift from energy to matter takes place, you begin to lose bits of yourself. Then suddenly you burst forth into life, you are born. You bring with you a sense of your own power. After all, you did get here, didn't you? You also bring with you the ability to love and be loved. You know this to the core of your being. This knowledge is visceral and intuitive, and no matter how far from this truth you move, there is always a secret knowing and a secret yearning to be in touch with it. It never completely goes away.

But as you have seen, and may remember, a child's life becomes a series of events and entanglements that begin to warp your trust and natural expression. It can be as apparently inconsequential as not being comforted when you cry. You begin to collect thought and behavior patterns and make life-informing rules based on your inability to accurately interpret the events and the experiences that make up your little life. You are not good at this job. You have been born unprepared for interpretation. As you separate from yourself, the world around you begins to define who you are. The Impostor is who you become—the one who does all of the things necessary to survive a world that can be harsh or cold.

It's essential to understand where and how your sense of self was created and where the Impostor took its identity. If you review the events and moments that you discovered behind the doors in the Corridor Visualization, you will begin to see how your sense of who you are formulates the Impostor.

For a friend of mine, an actor from England, the first corridor door that he opened revealed an event so deep and dark that he himself did not remember it until the visualization brought it forth. He was very small, perhaps three. He loved his grandfather very much and was often kept by him when his mum, who was raising him by herself, had to work at night. His grandfather would hold and cuddle him and he felt safe. Then one day the cuddling took a decided turn. He felt his little body being caressed in a new way. Fear began to replace the trust. As time went on, the caressing turned to abuse, and terror replaced the fear. Knowing his grandfather was a loving man, John decided that he was bad and that he deserved to be hurt; that pain was the price you paid for being bad and for being loved. The visualization revealed to him that his Impostor was a person who thought he deserved to be hurt, who lived in fear.

Susan, another friend of mine, opened a door to find herself in a closet. It was dark and she was lonely. She was shivering with cold and fear, and beyond the closet she heard shouts and cries. This closet was where she would hide when her father would come home drunk and beat her mother. She would huddle in this closet while she berated herself for being too afraid and too helpless to save her mother. These feelings pursued her through her entire life. It's probably no surprise that she is now a social worker, still trying to make up for not saving her mother by saving others.

It's easy to confuse who you are with the circumstances of your life. It is easier to take your identity from the input around you than to hold on to your Genuine Self. Often the world assaults you with its feedback. I saw a textbook example in a grocery store in New York, years ago.

There was an enormous woman pushing one of those oversized carts, spilling over with enough groceries to feed the Third World. Many children were hanging from one part or another of her anatomy or clothing, or trailing noisily after her. She did not appear to be having a good day. The smallest of this horde of little ones was tucked in the front of the cart between a loaf of bread and some toilet paper. As the woman stopped to choose some jelly, the youngest sibling reached its tiny hand out and grabbed a jar of jam; naturally, being too big for the little fingers to grasp, it slipped to the floor and broke with a loud crash. The woman went berserk! In a ballistic reaction she gave the child a wallop and began to shake him, screaming, "You are bad! You are bad! You are nuthin' but bad!" That's what the child heard over and over, and I sensed this was not the first time.

The child was not bad, in fact. He was a good child who dropped a jar of jam because it was too large for his little hand, and he had a mother whose life seemed unfulfilling; whatever it was that had once warped her, now she was overwrought, unable to see reality or react responsibly.

There is a world of difference between being bad and dropping a jar of jam. But the little kid can only associate his behavior with who he is. The more this notion is reinforced, the more the child will think of himself as bad. When he grows up, his behavior will surely reflect what he has been taught about himself. He'll "be bad!" or spend his life trying to "be good."

Whether our lessons have been as dramatically severe as John's or Susan's or as relentlessly routine as that of the boy who reached for the jam, for most of us, our experience of safety and power and love grow warped and dysfunctional. And so we begin to lay down the law that informs the rest of our lives. We forget that we are "good," and so the Impostor begins to act out in response to the drama we grow up within. Our behavior begins to reflect this drama.

You are not your behavior, and yet it is hard to disassociate the self from action. When children do things that please grown-ups, they are told that they are good little boys or girls. So it appears that the way to be good is to do good deeds and please others. This leaves you constantly trying to figure out how to "be" good. Since your only tip-off is the reaction of those around you, you are always on edge, at the mercy of other's reactions for your sense of self and worth. The groundwork is laid for feeling inadequate and "bad."

It takes a lot of work for a kid to live up to being good. It seems really easy to "be bad" or inconsiderate, or ungrateful or rude. Kids are experts at those things. They are reminded of how badly they act or behave. The truth, however, is that they are intrinsically good little people who sometimes, even often, behave badly, stupidly, inconsiderately, or ungratefully.

It isn't easy to figure out who you are when you are a kid. Your worldview is more than likely skewed by the worldview of those around you. I remember the last bit of personal vision that I had as a little girl before I disappeared into the system that my Impostor had set up for me. I had a vision that I would be someone important and that I would be loved; my role model was Wonder Woman. I just assumed that when I grew up I would be heroic and have something to do with making the world a safe place to live in. Then I began to be taught what it was that real little girls wanted and what it would be like when I became a woman. I was a slow learner. I took some convincing.

I was always on the side of the underdog and the rebel. As I championed each cause my parents would say, "Honey, you can't save the world!" Their words hurt, but I remember looking down at the invisible bullet-stopping bracelets on my wrists and muttering under my breath, "We'll just see about that!" And so the Wonder Woman I always wanted to be was always in conflict with the system that created the Impostor, the proper, subservient, and hyperrealistic American girl. Eventually, Wonder Woman slipped into oblivion and was replaced with a mild-mannered girl who did girl things and followed the rules.

In retrospect, it seems that when I let go of the Wonder Woman fantasy, I was left with the more subtle aspects of her character, aspects that suited the system I was creating to live by. First of all she was only effective when being superhuman. She was a loner who was looked up to but had no intimate relationships. She took on the task of saving the planet. Perfect! She found peers among the inhabitants of a mythological kingdom of women far from the activity of the mundane world. In order to get along in the "real" world, Wonder Woman had to divest herself of power and assume the identity of a secretary, one of the roles allotted to women at the time. That's pretty much how I did it. In the secret reaches of my heart I knew that the world I was living in wasn't real for me, so I sealed the door and the Impostor learned all of the social skills and graces that were appropriate.

The Impostor thrives according to the rules that are set down when we are children in development. The dreams of childhood are sealed away behind the doors of the practical necessity of surviving in a world that has little room for individuality and creativity. When your childhood vision began to threaten the system you were handed a rule book, with which you were to curb your disturbing reality and bring it into line. These rules inform adult behavior and keep adults from realizing their dreams.

The Impostor's Rules for Survival

How can a small child be at fault, when a parent has picked him up off his feet and is slugging him with their fists? But I believed it was me. And I grew up holding on to that idea. I made a rule out of it. I wrapped it in concrete and nobody could convince me otherwise.

Patrick France, *Los Angeles, 1986*

THE IMPOSTOR LIVES BY THE RULES. Those rules perpetuate your addiction to your personal drama. Chances are, if your father told you that you'd never amount to anything, you've made it a rule. If you were told that you couldn't make it on your own, you have a rule that you need someone in order to make it. Nice girls don't . . . Big boys don't . . . If you have something wonderful it will deprive someone else . . . It's your job to make sure that everyone is happy . . . It is easier for a camel to get through the eye of a needle than for a rich man to get into heaven . . . Put others first . . . Never let your guard down, or you'll be hurt . . . Be invisible . . . Never let anyone see your real feelings . . . People will take advantage of you . . . Never feel too deeply . . . You deserve to be hurt . . . Be afraid of people who aren't like you . . . No pain, no gain . . . I need a man to be worthwhile.

The variety of the Impostor's rules is endless, and no one's rules are likely to exist in exactly the same combination. Once, in a workshop about family of origin issues, Sudie Cunnane, a nurse and painter, and I were able to create quite a list of rules that she was unconsciously held by. She began by saying, "Yes, but I'm always going to have a certain amount of conflict in my life." I went to a flip chart and wrote that down, labeling it RULE #1. As she laughed at herself, she said, "Okay, okay. But my vulnerability and weakness will always get me into conflict." As I went to the chart to put this one down and label it RULE #2, the whole room began to chuckle. When I finished she said, "Yeah, but

I can't just have it the way that I want it. Oh! Rule number three, huh?" And so it was. In the space of a few moments she could see several rules that were limiting her, that kept her stuck. And she felt this way after recovery from substance abuse and major work on codependency. The Impostor can't live in a rule-free environment.

The Impostor may even have given you rules that conflict with each other, and so you've spent a lifetime in confusion trying to honor both sets. Let's say you grew up with mixed responses: one parent told you that you were swell, and the other beat you. This creates two complete systems of rules.

Sometimes the Impostor works in tricky ways. Sometimes the rules are so basic we miss them, such as a rule that we are bottom-line unworthy. All kinds of lesser rules may spring from that core rule, but "worthless" may at first seem too basic to understand as a rule.

Christopher Flynn, who was the dance coach and choreographer who had such a great impact on Madonna, said in that same workshop that he had grown up in so many foster homes that he didn't have time to inherit any rules. As we spoke it became clear that in order to survive, he had needed to figure out what the deal was in each home and to act accordingly. Without too much digging, he unearthed the rule that he must always be a chameleon. He always had to be able to camouflage himself, wherever he was; he had to "pass" as whatever he was surrounded by. He began to see just how much he had been forced to sacrifice of his self-expression for the sake of his own survival.

A woman who did a workshop that I led in London rediscovered a forgotten incident through a visualization. She had created a rule about herself that had shaped her sense of worth, and kept her forever striving to be noticed and to be good enough. She was two years old, in the corner of the living room, playing with blocks. Her four-year-old sister was playing with dolls quite near the front door, with the six year old reading next to her. Mom was in the kitchen preparing dinner. A lovely, proper British family. The key turned in the lock. Daddy was home! Dad picked up and hugged the one closest to the door, then the second child. As he did so, the phone rang. Mom called out from the kitchen that her hands were wet and asked him to get the phone. Being a good guy he did, and inadvertently overlooked giving our littlest "victim" her hug and kiss hello. From that moment she set it in stone that she wasn't as deserving as others and she'd have to prove that she was. All that actually happened was that the phone rang and Dad got sidetracked. It went unnoticed by everyone, and life went on as usual, but not really.

Now, you may think that was too insignificant to matter, so unintentional, so misinterpreted. Certainly it is very different from a childhood incest memory, and less painful to relive. Yet for this woman it was no less life-informing. The result, not the intensity of the event, is the point. And so rules are made up that guide our every step. They become part of our addictive cycle.

Imagine that you have a version of one of those books called *Rules of the Road* that your Department of Motor Vehicles gives out—only these are the rules that childhood sets down, and so no matter what road you take or how different the terrain, the rules still apply. You can change homes, work, lovers, countries, you can even get plastic surgery, and still the rules apply. I actually did that once—the plastic surgery part. When I was a teenager, I got my nose fixed. I thought it would change my life. All it changed was my nose. I liked my new nose, but I still hated my life. All of the rules I had been living by still applied.

It is one thing to correct something because you don't like it. It is quite another to correct yourself because you feel that you are not all right. All that will get fixed is the nose, the butt, the bod. The same rules will apply and the Impostor will continue to thrive. The problem is much more than skin-deep. It is as deep as childhood, and that is where the work needs to be done. We need to change the rules.

What are your rules of the road? There are a million things that you do over and over, and things that you always say. These are good clues. Just watch yourself go through the day following your own rules. They have been put in place to make sure that you stay in your place. As long as you do, the addiction to your drama is secure. Your belief system is unthreatened. It doesn't have to worry that the genuine you will emerge.

Once you see some of the rules that form the systems you operate within, you can begin to see how much your system resembles the malfunctioning systems that bred you. You can see how much of what you heard as a child is echoed in your own adult words. *These are rules that you unconsciously committed to and that invade the very spirit of your growing up and sap the strength of your adult creativity and spontaneity.*

Why not take out your journal and begin to examine the rules that guide your life? This is a good thing to use a journal for. You can begin by looking at where you are most stuck in your life. Ask yourself questions such as these.

- What is it that you are trying to do or to have? What's really in the way?
- Is it something that's been in the way other times?
- How do you feel about yourself?
- Have you felt this way before?
- Are you trying to do something that breaks a rule that you don't even know you've been living by?
- What precedent would be broken if you got what you wanted?
- What do you fear would happen if you got what you wanted?
- What were you told or what did you see as a child that would make this so?

It is important to remember that the Impostor invokes these rules and stumbling blocks in order to stay alive at the expense of your Genuine Self. If you are to emerge, you will have to break some time-honored rules. It is difficult to do so because these rules form the basis of the survival behavior that gets you through childhood, but quite covertly impedes your adult happiness. The first rules that need to be broken are those that are etched in stone and stand between you and fulfilling your commitment to your well-being.

When you grow, the world is fraught with dangers to your emotional and often physical well-being; you become a survivor. When the rules of your childhood tell you that the world is a dangerous place, and that to be vulnerable leads to being hurt, you will find a way to survive without being vulnerable. When you form a childhood rule that reality is too painful, you will create mechanisms to reinforce the rule and survive by shifting your reality. When your reality doesn't fit that of the adults around you, you will follow the rules of their reality in order to survive.

Survival isn't enough to thrive on, but it seems safe. As you grow you develop a set of coping skills to honor the rules and to help you survive the things that separate you from your Genuine Self. You suppress your feelings, you disregard your instincts, and the Impostor replaces the true loving self that you feel separate from. Employing all the denial you need, you create behavior that will allow you to adapt and endure. You begin to do this so early that you don't know you've done it. You become a survivor. You then become addicted to survival.

Let's look at how this dynamic works: Something happens in childhood—a major or minor event that separates you from your Genuine Self. You make a rule about it, and in order to survive, you develop a dysfunctional behavior that becomes automatic. In order to begin to release this behavior, it is necessary to trace it to its origins. To do this, let's return to the corridor from the first visualization to discover where you make your unconscious or conscious decisions about survival.

Reconnect to the energies from the center of the earth
  and the infinite universe.
In the space you've created let the corridor take shape.
Recognize it as the corridor that informed your childhood.
Now go back to the experiences and people that are behind these
  doors.
The ones that helped to create the Impostor.
The ones that created the need for survival.
Other events may appear that did not before.
Learn from them, they are showing up for a reason.
Just recognize them and explore what they have to offer.

Go to the first door.
Look around.
See where you are, who is there.
Take a deep breath and connect to the experience going on.
Let your breath flow through your body.
Let yourself feel the way you did then.
What did you realize about survival?

*How did you decide that you would be able to survive life in the
world?*

*Let the realization become physical
and for a moment see how it has affected you ever since.*

What did it feel like then?

Let your body have that experience.

How did you make it through?

Did something in you close off?

*For a moment allow yourself to become aware
of how that rule has affected your life.*

How has that childhood survival skill grown with you?

How does it direct you now?

*When you have the information that you need,
go to the door and prepare to leave that space and time.*

*Take a deep, deep breath and let the experience permeate your
body, then go through the door and release the images with a
sound.*

Do this repeatedly as you go down the corridor.

*As the connections become clear and when you have had enough,
bring your consciousness and awareness back to the present.*

*The old need to survive can become the chains of your personal prison. The
prison is your belief system, and one of those beliefs is that you need the tools that
you developed in the past to survive the present.*

I would suggest that you write down in your journal what you have
discovered, and make sure that you keep breathing deeply so that you
are present in your body and do not go to your mind to sort things out.
(It is very powerful to see this stuff on paper.) Your Impostor may try
to talk you out of doing this. Right now is a good time to allow it to
know that you are in charge.

To summarize: your adult life is spent reenacting the malfunction you developed in childhood. You are hooked on this stuff. We all have our own rules of the road, our own set of commandments, which offer as little flexibility, substance, and freedom as the ones that were handed down in ancient times and reinterpreted to suit the needs of every malfunctioning system since Moses. Where Moses feared to walk, we now run!

Mastering the Present

Mastering the Present

The trick for me, as I look at all of the things that I have done habitually over the last thirty-odd years, is not to beat myself up for having done them. When I was a kid I would beat myself up all the time for fucking up. That way I could empathize with my father, who beat me. I finally have no more abusers in my life unless I fall into that old pattern and do it to myself.

Robert Redding, *Los Angeles, 1986*

MASTERING THE PRESENT MEANS THAT YOU MOVE FROM ADDICTIVE, HABITUAL SURVIVAL TO A LIFE OF CHOICE. When you make this move you will confront the core addiction to your personal drama. You will then begin to find ways to allow your life to flow organically from within, keeping you in relationship with, not subject to, the outside world. You will live simply within the truth, breaking old patterns and rules. In a sense you will surrender, trusting that there is something with which to replace your malfunctioning systems. Once you develop that trust, you can begin to create a new and integrated way to experience yourself and life. New and integrated. A kind of *whole* living.

Mastering the present is about recognizing the relationship between your present behavior and the core addiction that thrives on the drama and the belief systems that were created in your childhood. Mastering the present confronts the relationship between your childhood and how your childhood patterns are replicated in adulthood. It revises the relationship between your Impostor and your Genuine Self. Once you are clear on how these relationships interact and the way your past is expressed in your present, you will be ready to begin a process of repair so your Genuine Self can emerge.

You can immediately begin to repair *your relationship to control and denial.* When you were a kid, whatever control you could exert was a way to keep disaster at bay, and so being in control at any cost has always seemed like a good idea. That is far from the truth. A need to control is a message from your Impostor.

Denial is one of the most important survival tools that you possess. It is an attempt to control reality. It allowed you to get through childhood. It presently allows all sorts of other survival techniques to go on unnoticed or justified. It will allow you to be abused, to be in relationships that don't work, to allow totally unacceptable behavior to become acceptable, to take care of people who should be taking care of themselves, to smother and call it love. Denial will allow you to accept a lie and to assume that the path you are on is the right one.

There are lots of exercises that will enable you to begin to untie the knots that bind you firmly to your history and suppress a creative, satisfying, rapturous life in the present. You will not only have an opportunity to see more clearly the mechanism that the Impostor uses to stay alive and to perpetuate the system, but you will be given some tools to make it safe for your Genuine Self to come through. Those tools, appearing here as exercises and visualizations, are to be used as you see fit. Use the ones that seem relevant, and above all, use the ones that seem scary. The more that you put yourself firmly into the process, the easier the process will become. I know that it sometimes seems overwhelming and impossible, but it really isn't. An acting student of mine once said to me as he was working through a major life change, "I'm really on the right track, but there's stuff in my behavior that doesn't know what to do yet!" Give yourself a little grace period. It takes time for your behavior to shift; after all, what you are doing is recovering from your core addiction. What lies at the end of this exploration is a freedom that will allow your intuitions to become your guide as you master the present.

Confronting the Core Addiction

O*ne day I looked around at all of the chaos that I was growing up in, and even though I was a little kid, I swear I said to myself, "Am I really the only one who is crazy around here?" I think it gave me a little bit of perspective on life. Just a little bit, mind you!*

Herman Alvarez (Diva), *Los Angeles, 1986*

ABOUT FIFTEEN YEARS AGO I WAS GOING TO A WONDERFUL THERAPIST IN NEW YORK WHO OFFERED ME AN INSIGHT THAT WAS SO POWERFUL THAT I LEFT THERAPY. I'd gone for help to try to make myself fit into my marriage, and later to fit into my divorce. One day I was railing on and on about how awful I was and how I was never going to fit in, how hopeless I was, how I was never going to fix myself. Suddenly, my therapist, who seemed like the perfect human being to me, began to laugh and laugh. I found this very alarming. I asked her what was so funny and she began to laugh harder! Now I was really beginning to panic. The person I trusted with my very sanity was losing it; and besides, I hated to be laughed at. She finally managed to utter a few words between heaving breaths. "You are crazy!" she exclaimed.

These were not words that I was longing to hear. "Isn't that what you are trying to fix?" I asked.

When she finally composed herself, she explained that what she had been laughing at was her realization that what I wanted to fix was the wrong thing. It was true that I didn't seem to fit in, but that wasn't the problem. The problem was that I kept *trying* to fit in. I was trying to get rid of all of my uniqueness, all of my creativity, and all of my own needs in order to fit in. What needed to be fixed was not me, but my desire to fix me!

I had just been given permission to be myself, whoever that was. I had been given permission to look life in the eye and see who was reflected back and to give up the pain of living as an Impostor. Still, I wasn't quite ready. My core addiction to my personal belief system—that there was something wrong with me—still gripped me. The idea of letting go was unthinkable. The system won again, as it does for so many until the time comes when you have no choice but to break away.

Keeping the idea of the core addiction in mind, I begin most of my workshops with the question "How many of you are in therapy, are therapists, or both?" Hands fly up, and the sound of laughter slowly begins to fill the space. "Keep them up. Now of those with your hands down, how many have been in a spiritual or recovery program or done transformational or some such seminars?" More hands fly up. I have them look around the room to discover that the addition of this category covers almost everyone in the hall. When my own hand gets tired from being raised, we go to work.

The next thing I ask is for each of us to consider if it makes sense that there is something wrong with all of us. Does it make sense that we come into the world basically flawed and unable to cope? Could it really be possible that humankind is intended to be nothing but a roster of character defects that begin to roll forth at birth? What is it that we are always trying to fit into?

It seems as if we are all trying to get better, to fit into some sort of structure or system. Since everyone has to "work" so hard to fit into the system, it just might be that the system doesn't work. The problem, then, could lie not with us, but with the structure. That would explain why we consistently find ourselves, particularly in the growing up process, at odds with the system. This could explain why it is next to impossible to feel normal, and why in fact we have become addicted to feeling abnormal, out of sync, not enough.

"Normal" is a set of rules that were devised irrespective of human nature, human need, and humanity. A conformity to someone else's lifestyle code. An idealized and impossible morality that has clearly defined limits, and guarantees a struggle to conform. When I look back to what little childhood I can remember, every time I felt out of place or unloved it was because I was doing what came naturally and ran smack into some wall that had "Don't even try it!" written all over it. For most of us this holds true as adults as well. We are so used to running into the walls of our self-separation that we don't know we've built them. If no one in the world around us limits us, we will limit ourselves. It is habitual.

A man I worked with in San Francisco said to me, "When I was a kid, no matter what I did, I still didn't know what was going to happen at home. Some days I was safe, and everybody seemed happy, and other days were a cross between a violent nightmare and a dime novel. It amazes me that when I take a good look at my day-to-day life, it's still pretty much the same. I've worked on it, and it looks better, but I can't let go of the way it's always been. It's like I'm hooked on it!"

Over the years I have worked with people to guide them to their own power. We worked on substance abuse and codependence. We worked on obsessive behavior. We worked on letting go of the past, of blame, of guilt. We worked on letting go of old patterns of dysfunction and survival. We worked on being in the present and letting themselves off the hook. In that way we began to confront their core addictions in a manner that recovery programs or therapy so often cannot.

But I began to see a pattern emerge even within this process. There was just so much genuine recovery or self-love a person could handle. There always came a time when things seemed to be going too well, when there was a "danger" of having life work, when the core addiction was too threatened. Then something would happen. Something would trigger the old stuff again. Like an alcoholic who slips, you're back there again in the drama.

A man in Los Angeles had been doing a lot of work on himself. He had just begun to deal with the fact that the happiness in his big Italian family was an illusion. They were, in fact, monstrously unkind to one another. He was in the process of putting his Catholicism and his desperate need for approval into perspective. He was seeing that his life was run by trying to be enough for everyone. His control obsession was honed down to a fine art. When people got too close he would find a way to shut them out. But he made a mistake. You see, he had found his way to a group of people who accepted him unconditionally, who really loved him. He didn't need to "be" any particular way for them, and they didn't need him to "do" anything for them.

This was too much for him to take. It broke the one rule he was truly addicted to: the rule of the Impostor, the result of the malfunctioning past, the system of self-deprecation that he grew up with. Only by clinging desperately to his addictive drama could he remain self-loathing in the face of all the love around him. He chose the self-loathing the way an addict takes a fix. He knew he was at a point where the reality around him no longer treated him like the hateful child he thought he was. The reality around him reflected a powerful, lovable, deserving man with free choice. The jig as up! The choice before him was to embrace reality, which would have meant to embrace true recovery.

In one group session he sat at a table literally clinging to its edge as if he were clinging physically to his past. I watched this man begin to turn red from the strain of holding on. He could not let go. His knuckles whitened as he clung to the vestiges of his history. His Impostor was clearly fighting for its life.

His core addiction was raging. He was addicted to his pain, his drama, his past. He was used to it. He was used to thinking he was awful, addicted to his shame. It took a very long time for him to be willing to look at the possibility that he had grown up abused and vilified and that he had now taken on that task for himself. Once he could look at that reality, he was able to begin to see that others did not find him worthy of abuse. It was with gentle, patient prodding that the group began to help him break free. He started to accept himself and see through to the promise that the world once held out to him.

An executive who took one of my workshops as her tenuous grip on her company was slipping said righteously that she was the only one at her company who had never been addicted to anything. As if she weren't addicted to her righteousness! She was also run by her need to control, her elitism, and the distance that she placed between herself and others. She didn't have a clue. She denied totally that her life had become unmanageable because of these traits.

In fact, she exhibited all of the character traits of an addict. She was constantly covering up mistakes, because it wasn't all right for her to make them. She was a perfectionist, so when she made a mistake or did something unsuccessfully she lied to the board of directors, she lied to her staff, and she lied to herself. She always blamed others for the ramifications of her behavior. Doesn't it sound just like the cycle of substance abuse, without the substance?

It turned out that this woman had grown up in a family where substances were abused and so were family members. She survived by being perfect and never creating a problem. She learned the art of manipulation as a survival mechanism and turned denial into high art. Everything always had to look good. She learned charm. She could lie without batting an eyelash. She became a perfect sociopath, working her craft.

She was run by her unresolved childhood just like any good old drunk. The acting out of her core addiction was just easier to deny because it was less visible. For people in this state, it is themselves and others that they abuse rather than a substance. She was intransigent and unwilling to admit that the core addiction existed. She was too committed to her denial and her need to think she was in control. She went on to another company, where she will no doubt repeat the behavior she was unwilling to confront.

The confrontation with your core addiction is crucial to the growth process. Once you confront the addiction, it is also important to acknowledge that no matter how full our lives become, the Impostor is just waiting in the wings to make another entrance. We are addicts. We are addicted to our history and our drama. No matter what internal or external changes we make, we must fight falling off the wagon, returning to an old pattern, denying reality, forgetting that life can be full and exciting without drama. I use Alcoholics Anonymous to keep me present. If I am not vigilant, I might forget that I'm not the same old girl I used to be, that in fact I never was that girl, I only thought that I was. I also know that it is as important to stay vigilant when things are wonderful as when they are rough.

Hindsight bathes my history in the light of reality. I had lived a lifelong series of dramatic episodes, repeating the same behavior over and over, in different guises. Knowing that I was on a treadmill and that it acted, for me, just like any other addictive cycle allowed things to get easier. It allowed me to experience who I really am. I am a powerful, deserving, loving woman, and I am a drama addict.

Breaking Dysfunctional Behavior Patterns

Why do I have a feeling I've done all of this before? I've had this relationship before, I've had this conversation before. It's sort of déjà vu, but not the psychic kind!

Ted Karavidas, *Boston, 1989*

As YOU GROW UP, YOU TURN EXPERIENCES AND THE RULES THAT YOU LIVE BY INTO THE BASIS FOR YOUR BEHAVIOR. In other words, you base expectations on past events and respond to them the way you did in the past. If a rat in a maze knows cheese is placed at the end of a tunnel, it will go for the cheese. After a few successes, the rat will go for the cheese even if it isn't hungry. The rat goes into the tunnel; the familiarity triggers its behavior. It salivates and automatically goes for the cheese without regard to hunger or obstructions or any of the other things that involve choice.

Now, because we have minds and choice, unlike rats, you would naturally assume that human beings do not respond in the same way to stimuli. Wrong! We do. We respond to things in the present that trigger a rule from the past. We follow the pattern we have set. Something triggers certain sensations, and we respond in a way that is coded and part of the pattern. A stimulus creates an expectation, the expectation sets the code of our rule, and we're off and running. The behavior follows the rule. These are the mechanics of a pattern.

It is true that we, as humans, do not do this quite the way rats do. Rats have a better sense of reality. A rat will only go through a maze five times on automatic after not finding any cheese as a reward. A rat has a better sense of "that was then, this is now" than humans.

To achieve any Mastery over the present, you have to unravel the threads of the veil that your Impostor uses to shroud your power. To unravel these threads, you need to continually take a hard look at your behavior patterns. These patterns are protectors of the system that has warped you and caused you to malfunction.

When you go into pattern mode, the rat-maze mode, Mastery of the present slips from your grasp. You may have a lot of trouble telling when you are falling into a pattern. But every time you hear yourself say, "This always happens," you are most likely being run by an old pattern. "This never happens" is the reverse of the same syndrome. If your results are always the same, if you feel that you have been down the same road before, if you run into a wall and never seem to get beyond it, chances are that the wall was built long ago; and every time you re-create a similar situation, the wall gets thicker and harder to get beyond. Every time you get close to breaking a rule of the system, the automatic behavior sets in.

When you are running a behavior pattern, or I should say being run *by* one, you are out of touch with the fact that you have many choices. You forget that there are options in any set of circumstances. Here is the technology: you come up against a circumstance or person that triggers a feeling and some expectations from childhood. In order to survive in childhood you set up some rule, and now you react habitually in a way that follows that rule.

Paul, an actor that I have counseled, said that acting class was very painful for him, more so than auditions. So was the rehearsal process of getting a show on its feet. He said that in class and in rehearsal he always felt inept and inadequate. Criticism seemed life-threatening. When he became afraid, he couldn't hear what he was being told and so could never quite get things right, further enhancing his terror. Often he would bolt from class or leave a production, undermining his career.

When Paul was a little boy, his dad spent weekends fixing things that were in ill repair around the house, and in order to be with his dad, Paul would try to learn to fix things. His dad was highly critical and Paul could never get things quite right. His father would always let loose a torrent of criticism, sometimes beat him, and when Paul felt too threatened he would run from the house to the woods, where he felt safer. As an adult he turned his teachers and directors into his dad, and if they criticized his work, the feelings of childhood and the desire to run would arise.

If you were constantly told as a kid that you would amount to nothing, chances are you made up a rule around it. You may have accepted it as an accurate assessment of your place in the world or may spend your life trying to prove that you can make it. Neither approach will create satisfaction for you. Neither is about what you really want.

A film producer that I know began to measure his success by the hit shows and money that he accumulated. This makes sense, since that's the usual measure of success, or making it. His parents had died before his success became apparent and yet he still seemed to be motivated by a fierce desire to prove to himself that they had been wrong about him.

Though he was raking in the bucks, had two homes, great cars, great trips, and was courted by everyone, he was not happy. What he really wanted to do was have an impact on society, but he could not adjust his picture of success to accommodate his passion. He was unwilling to run the risk of using his craft to follow his passion. That would have required taking enormous risks and perhaps producing shows that would not yield great box office receipts or be popular hits. His pattern was to prove himself, and so he would continue to do so at the expense of his happiness.

A man from New York talks about being the leader of a tricycle gang when he was small. The kids would get together and ride like the wind, pedaling their little hearts out. Like the head of a mini "Wild Bunch," he'd always be out in front, wildly out of control, feeling free and joyous, until one day he ran smack into a fire hydrant. He was badly hurt. As he picked himself up off the ground and looked down at his bloody knees, a rule rose up for him: it's too dangerous to be out in front. It is not safe to lead. Without knowing it, he set limits for his growth. Every time the chance for leadership presented itself, he would automatically sabotage it in some way. Whenever he felt out of control, or what others might call free, he would hold back. A major factor of his life was determined by a fire hydrant.

Similarly, codependence is a behavior pattern established in childhood. Many people can't define themselves without someone to need them. Codependents are drawn to caregiving in droves. Many caregivers are unaware that this pattern exists. They don't understand why they burn out and receive little satisfaction from their work, but they can't fill the unmet needs of childhood with good deeds in the present. It just doesn't work that way. If a child has a rule that she could earn love by caring for siblings or an alcoholic parent, she sets up the pattern of trying to earn love by being needed. Such a person can't realize she's earned the right to be loved by simple virtue of her birth.

If nobody paid attention to you when you were a kid unless you were in trouble, you may have made it a behavior rule, and thus have continued to develop very sophisticated negative attention-getting techniques. But the kind of attention you get will only act to activate your drama and self-loathing, reinforcing your separation from your Genuine Self.

Here is a subtle behavior pattern that I think warps many of us. If we were able to feel love and get attention by getting sick, we may have established a lifelong health pattern quite unbeknownst to us. When we are feeling lonely and unloved we may suddenly become ill, summoning up a lot of attention and caring. We are unaware that our need for attention has come about through an old childhood survival technique. If we hated school and discovered that we didn't have to go if we were sick, it could have established an automatic pattern of getting ill to avoid an unpleasant situation.

The insidious things about behavior patterns is that they often work. If you took care of the adults in your family in order to be loved and you felt loved, the behavior worked. If you were able to get attention by getting into trouble and you needed attention, the behavior worked. If you got what you wanted when you got sick, the behavior worked. After a while it probably stopped working, but the behavior became automatic—so now when you want someone to be close and caring, you get sick.

Obsessive, compulsive, and addictive behaviors are clearly patterns, but what is not so clear to addicts is that *the addiction is the response to a deeper pattern. An addiction is a way to cope with life. It is a response to one basic rule: life is too painful. When we stop engaging in the addictive and compulsive behavior patterns, we are then faced with the underlying behavior patterns that the addiction has been masking.*

The first step in overcoming your behavior patterns is to recognize that some of them actually helped you for a while. If being invisible as a kid kept you from being killed, it was a good idea. If being smart kept you from being hurt, it was a good idea. The problem is that you can't determine when a good idea becomes a bad habit. John Mordaunt, a man living with AIDS in the United Kingdom, a writer, and an AIDS activist, said, "I wanted to be an addict! I know it sounds weird, but I did! On my thirteenth birthday a friend turned me on. The minute the needle went into my arm, all of the insecurities, all of the ugliness went away. It was the first time in my life I didn't feel ashamed to be me."

A child doesn't set out to be a closed-off, shut-down adult with an intimacy problem. A codependent doesn't set out to become addicted to other people's reality and dependence for his or her own security. When you get your self-worth from winning enough awards, doing the right thing, getting acknowledgment, it seems like a good idea. People do not consciously choose to be victims. They intend simply to survive and to feel better.

When I had my first line of cocaine, I didn't say, "Wow! Now I'm on the road to chemical dependency! Now I can put major portions of my income up my nose and feel separate, disassociated, and tense!" I didn't consciously set out to become high-strung, lockjawed, sleepless, and fried. I set out to feel smart, to fit in, to have more energy, and to add a few hours to my day.

The initial instinct that leads to addiction—the instinct to feel good and to feel good about yourself—is valid and powerful. It is a wonderful notion and means that on a very deep level you know you deserve to feel good. You know you are worthy and you want to be in touch with that worthiness.

In the film *Night of the Hunter,* Robert Mitchum plays a preacher who has *HATE* tattooed on one hand and *LOVE* on the other. He joins his hands and arm wrestles good and evil. Here is the self (love) and here too is the addiction (hate). *Your instinct to survive and feel good about yourself can be honored and used as a way to honor your commitment to your well-being.* What also becomes apparent is that the substance abuse and other dysfunctional patterns that we have used to feel good, like the ones that we have used to follow the rules set down in childhood, only perpetuate the core addiction.

You cannot be in touch with the self from anywhere but from within yourself. That is why dope, booze, awards, control, and hundreds of other survival tools leave you still separated from who you are. You try to honor the instinct to feel good by looking outside yourself for the feeling. It isn't to be found in anything external. It can only be found within the self.

The time has come to look at breaking the code on some of the essential pieces that keep our addictive selves on the treadmill. Since the cycle is habitual, let's look at breaking these habitual patterns.

What you need is a technology for breaking the patterns that keep you tied to the past and out of touch with living fully, powerfully, and lovingly in the present. To do this you can:

- Identify the patterns.
- See the ramifications of those patterns.
- Trace those patterns to their origins, as closely as possible, recognizing what really happened and separating reality from your interpretation.
- See what rules you made up and cast in stone.
- See what other choices might have been possible if you had been aware of reality.
- Now that you can make choices and are free of the pattern, find out what you can have in your life.

How do you identify your dysfunctional patterns? How do you see their ramifications? How do you get to the source of them?

All good questions. There are no absolute answers, but we will engage in a process for you to discover as much about those patterns as you can and are ready to at this time.

Find a comfortable place and play music if you like.
Begin to allow your breath to deepen.
Use whatever technique for entry into the visualization
    that works for you to awaken your consciousness.
Allow your breath to bring light into your body.
Allow your image to fill with that light.
The light of the truth.
Feel the light in your own body.
Let it radiate through you and beyond, filling your field of vision.
Just allow yourself to become part of the light . . .

What is it that you most want in the world?
How do you want your life to feel?

Why don't you have it that way?
Let the answer come from deep within you . . .
What stops you from being fulfilled?
Listen to the answer . . .
What does it feel like in your body right now?
Breathe into those feelings and let out a sound.
Let the feelings run through you . . .

Be aware of the pattern that has created the most powerful wedge
between you and having what you want in the world.
Let the pattern reveal itself to you . . .
Breathe through your body and see how you feel about looking
at this pattern.
Let out a sound.
If there is any resistance, breathe through it.
Let the awareness of the pattern and your feelings run through
you.

See yourself to be surrounded by light.
In the light begin to see yourself in a recent situation where the
pattern that keeps you from having what you want comes up.
Give yourself time and feel the experience . . .
Step into this recent experience when this pattern came up.
Who was there?
What was happening?
How do you feel about yourself/
See what it is that sets this pattern in motion.
What's the thought?
What's the feeling?
What sets you off into this automatic behavior?
What does it feel like?
Does it feel familiar?

Let yourself understand the impact of the moment . . .
Let your whole body reexperience it . . .
What are the ramifications of this behavior?
What are the results?
Is it what you wanted?
Is it what you expected?
What always happens?
See what the impact is . . .
Stay in touch with the feelings and sensations, and when you are
    ready, let the images fade away.

Keep breathing into those feelings and sensations
    and allow images of a time long ago when this pattern began.
If you can get to the very first time that would be brilliant.
Otherwise just go where you are taken.
See yourself, early on.
What happens?
It isn't even a pattern yet.
Something happens and you feel a certain way and respond a cer-
    tain way.
What is it that happens?
How do you feel?
Let your body experience the moment.
See whatever it is that triggers the behavior
    and feel the profound impact it has on your body and your life.
Watch yourself in the behavior and its limitation.
What decisions did you make about yourself and the world around
    you?
What did you decide?
What did you cast in stone?
What did it feel like in your body?
This is the pattern that has trapped you.
See the reality of the moment.

*Allow yourself to see the reality and decisions that have trapped
  you.*

*See if there were other things that, had you had the information
  or known how, you might have done.*

*What possibilities can you see now that you couldn't possibly have
  seen then?*

*Once you see that you can rewrite the script,
  you can see possibilities in the present . . .*

How might it have turned out differently?

*Use your imagination to see what you might have done
  and what might have happened if you could have had a
  choice . . .*

Begin to release the experience.

It was in the past.

It does not need to be relevant in the present.

Be willing to release the hold it has on you in the present.

*Breathe into the places in your body where you feel your power,
  your creativity, and your compassion.*

*Allow it to radiate through you,
  sweeping away your attachment to the pattern.*

See that right here, right now, there are many other choices.

See yourself in the present, filled with creativity and choice.

*How can you respond in the present
  and have your life reflect the way you want your life to be?*

Breathe deeply and let that go.

Come up with another way to respond, and another.

See how creative you can get.

How else might you respond and feel?

Allow the sense of possibility to flow through you.

*Keep breathing into your power and creativity
  and allow yourself to see other patterns.*

*Catch glimpses of other patterns that have limited your life and
  well-being.*

See the patterns that affect your health.
What are they?
Breathe through your body.
What about relationship patterns?
What other patterns lie between you and your well-being?
See them and know that you can come back to them
  whenever you want and release them as well.
Begin to feel what it might be like to live without these patterns.
As you see them, let them fall away.
As you release them, feel energy vibrating in your body.
Allow that energy to become light.
Feel yourself free!
In the light begin to see what life might feel like
  without being encumbered by the patterns that you are
  letting go!
Allow yourself to feel what it would be like.
What could you have?
What could you do?
Keep allowing the impact of the freedom on your body.
The openness, the joy.
You deserve it.
You are lovable and powerful and you can be free.

It is very important to free yourself from patterns that inhibit your joy and diminish your well-being and keep you from nurturing your Genuine Self. *These are our ties to the past put into action.* Your creativity can offer you options to these patterns. Recognition and choice can set you free.

With each of the patterns that you unearth, spend some time looking at what it is that you really want to happen in each case and how many options there are for moving toward that. I suggest that you keep breathing into your feelings as you do this and just let your imagination run wild. How could you do it differently from what has been dictated by the past? How could you frame your actions to respond to the present situation, even if the feelings from the past come up? What can you do to break the pattern and be in the moment?

It may be as simple as looking very clearly at a person whom you are interacting with and saying silently, "This is not my mother, father, the perpetrator who once wounded me . . ." "I know that when I was little and I said what I thought, I got hurt. This is me as an adult. I know I still feel like a kid, but the people who hurt me aren't here and there is no reason for these people to hurt me."

It may be that you will need to have a talk with yourself about your circumstances. "Well, everything that I want is just within reach and I know that I was told that I was no good and would never make it, but it's okay to break that rule. It's okay to make it." These are conversations that will help to bring you into the present and to let you see the options. When you have choice, there is freedom. And as you might have guessed, with freedom comes Mastery.

The Illusion of Control

I used to think that I was in control. I had it all handled. I had a great career, fabulous house, lots of friends, a lover who was my exact picture. I managed every aspect of my life so that it was the way I wanted it to be. I managed every memory. Now I will admit that this all was a bit stressful, but it seemed like that was a small price to pay for being on top of things! Then I got AIDS. It wasn't in my plan and I think that was harder for me to deal with than the disease itself.

Joe Manzio, *Los Angeles, 1987*

ONE OF THE MOST IMPORTANT ELEMENTS OF MASTERY IS TO RELEASE THE NEED TO BE IN CONTROL. In the acceptance of reality and the letting go of the need to control comes an amazing peace and freedom. When you are trying to control, you are not in the present, and you are not mastering some of your most deep-seated patterns, which exist around control issues.

Like Joe Manzio, many of us have had a try at surviving by being in control and manipulating reality. And like Joe, most of us, usually in less drastic ways than he, have come to see that we are not really in control. A major part of our lives is dedicated to trying. At best what we actually have is the illusion of control.

You can create an awareness of your own control mode by being in touch with what goes on in your body when it clicks in. Like any other dysfunctional behavior pattern, the need to control is activated by circumstances that bring up some childhood feelings of being *out* of control. See what it does to you. Let yourself get an idea of the cost of trying to be in control. Let yourself begin to recognize it when it happens.

Close your eyes and breathe deeply through your body.
Let your thoughts drift over the last few days.
Think about something or someone you have been trying to control.
What might you be trying to make happen?
Is there someone you are trying to change?
Some circumstances that you are trying to manipulate?
Some way you want people to think or act?
Give it a minute, you'll be able to find something . . .
What or who is it that you are trying to control?
Really think hard about what you are trying to control . . .
How are you trying to control things?
See yourself trying to control whatever or whoever it is . . .
How are you trying to control things?
What are you doing?

Breathe through your body and let out a sound.
Begin to be aware of the effect that it is having on your body.
See what happens in your body.
Really think hard.
Where do you feel the control?
Are you really in control or does your need to control have the power now?
Stay with it until you feel the impact.
When you are ready, let your breathing return to normal and your consciousness to the room.

Is this a nice thing to do to your body? And what good does it do, anyway? What you seek to control controls *you,* so what's the point? These are not frivolous questions. It is a function of growing up in the midst of malfunction that you try to control and resist any reality that does not serve your core addiction. It is a part of your survival behavior, and though it served you as a child, it can cause misery in adulthood.

Sometimes you control in the guise of service. It is a great mask for a codependent. You can resist feelings of unworthiness by doing good deeds. You can control and manipulate others by earning their love and making them need you. You can resist your own pain by focusing on the pain and well-being of others. Of course, until you break the cycle of resist and control, no one is being served, only your core addiction. You can deny your reality by participating in the reality of others.

If you have an alcoholic spouse you have to take care of him (or her). He will come home drunk and humiliated, and though you may be disgusted and yell at him, you will forgive him, hold him, put him to bed, and mend any bridges that he has burned. You will try to talk him into quitting, but will be understanding if he falls off the wagon. You will struggle to pay the bills. You will allow abuse because he is not himself. You will be his victim, his martyr. You are indispensable. You are in charge.

If you try to control others, your life becomes about domination, manipulation, and scheming. Just when you think you are on top of things, or people, whatever or whoever you have been trying to control will make a run for freedom. Perhaps the alcoholic actually recovers and doesn't need you anymore. You have lost control and have to face your own issues.

For some individuals, just controlling the people in their immediate lives isn't enough; they try it on a larger scale, in a corporation or in politics. Still, the illusion of control will only be temporary. The things that you try to control will eventually run riot.

Control is mistaken for power. This is a natural confusion, since those who once (when you were small) had control over you seemed to have all the power. It is important to note that this is not so. People who experience their own power don't need to control others.

The New Age, self-help, and fundamentalist religion games are full of leaders and stars who want to control *you.* They feel powerless on a deep, personal level, and so to serve their own denial and images, they develop quite subtle and effective means of exerting control over their disciples. First of all, their presentation is carefully controlled. They won't risk letting you know how needy they are for your approval, your worship, or your bucks. They need to control your sense of yourself as well, so that you will become dependent on their teachings.

They will manipulate the Scriptures they quote, the philosophies they espouse, and the jargon that they preach. They need you, and in order to keep you they have to make you think you need them. They too are controlled by their need.

The more you seek to control, the more controlled you are. It is a painful and isolating cycle. You try to make others see you the way you want them to, and respond to you the way you want them to, and the need to control drives a wall between you and them. You can't make someone feel about you the way that you want them to. You can't make someone see you in a certain light. You can't make someone love or respect you. When you seek to control another, all you can do is keep intimacy away. Your need for intimacy and your fear of it put you in a cycle of trying to control and being thwarted, thus reinforcing your sense of unworthiness.

Controllers may play a good game of being responsible because they are so often in charge, or the best helper ever, but in fact they are victims. When they are deprived of their sense of control they will do whatever it takes to get back into control, even at the sacrifice of their loved ones, the group that they head, or the vision they want to put forth in the world. Their control becomes more important than anything. When someone needs to be in charge, watch out! When you need to be in charge, watch out!

This doesn't mean that to be in charge means that you are a control freak. Many people run things because they have a vision to manifest, or because they are clearly the best at doing the job. Their identity and survival, however, are not at stake. They are not addicted to control.

I was unaware of how much I needed to be in control until I had a physical demonstration of it. I used to lead workshops called "On the Edge" in central Wales; they were a combination of metaphysical exploration and wilderness retreat. About thirty participants would look into themselves, confronting the issues that stood between them and having the richest possible experience of life. They then confronted physical realities that mirrored those issues.

This exercise was to be a surprise to me. Once layered and swathed in waterproofing, we set off for the river. The Welsh landscape was exquisite. The sound of the river came rushing into our ears. We began by walking along the bank. We were to follow the macho Welshman who owned the retreat site. Suddenly he began to walk *in* the river. I, not to be less macho, followed right behind, pretending no fear. Soon the water was waist deep. Soon it was deeper. He turned to us and said over the roar of the water that we would soon be unable to walk and that we were to "lean back, ass down, feetfirst and enjoy the ride." Enjoy the ride indeed! Going downstream, very fast, *out of control* is not my idea of a good time.

Let me tell you, ass down, feetfirst doesn't sit well with the mind, which is the part we are all used to leading with. Though in my innermost self, I felt safe and taken care of, and though I knew to be calm, my mind was going wild. So I tried to control the situation.

I lurched forward, leading with my brain, and tried to swim. I tried to control my flow down this river. As I did, I found that I was underwater one moment, being tossed against the rocks the next, banging into boulders, and swallowing and choking water, until I was *so* tired. Then I just lay back again—ass down, feetfirst.

The river was carrying me safely along its path. But still I thought I was doing the navigating, so I failed to notice that what I was struggling to create and control was already happening. When I realized that the river was working me rather than the other way around, I tried to control the river again. Once again I was tossed about mercilessly, hurled and bounced against rocks. Suddenly I saw what I was doing and just stopped, and resumed floating ass down, feetfirst, and allowed the flow to carry me safely and lovingly along. Ass down, feetfirst, that's my new mantra!

If you can surrender to the way the world works, you will not have to struggle. Work, yes—but struggle, no! I don't mean to suggest that you be passive, but painful, unhappy, unproductive struggle is a sign that perhaps your efforts are going in the wrong direction. When you keep doing something over and over and don't get the result you want, examine either the way you are going about your pursuit or the goal itself. You see, you can only do what is doable. The result is not in your control. So if you keep beating your head against a wall and the wall won't come down, perhaps it isn't meant to.

This doesn't mean that you should just lie back and wait. *It means that you should pay attention to reality rather than try to control or dominate it. Sometimes there is a greater plan at work.* A teacher named Lawrence was moving from California to New Mexico. He had shipped off all his things and was about to pile his cat, Sabrina, into the car and take the drive to his new home. He and his cat had been living in an apartment; they were headed to a house in the country. He picked up the cat to put her in the car. Now, this cat had only been in the car for trips to the vet, so she was afraid of the car. She assumed that he was taking her to get prodded and poked and frightened. The cat decided to take control of her destiny and bolted! It took the better part of the day to track down the cat and get her into the car. Remember, this cat was headed for a wonderful new home, a place where she could roam free and explore a whole new world. *There was a greater plan at work.* She just didn't know it.

So, keep working toward what you want, and trust that if it is supposed to come to you, it will. And trust that if you are on the wrong track, there will be red flags along the way. Trust is the key word. You don't have to struggle if you trust. Someone once said that worry and struggle are a breach of faith with God. If you read the signals, then you can manifest that which serves not only you but the greater good. You will be in alignment with the universe.

You can influence and allow and accept, but you cannot control. You cannot experience well-being by being in control. You cannot do it through manipulation, trying to create your own reality, or denial.

Then there is a whole series of things that you can affect and influence. You can have your say, state your preference, do your best. You can move others with your words, you can say how you want something to be—but ultimately the result is not within your province. I work hard for political candidates who stand for human rights and freedom. I make speeches and rally people to the cause. I can wax eloquent and be persuasive—but when my listeners go into the voting booth, they vote for the candidate of *their* choice, not necessarily *mine.* When you know this, you are free. All you can do is be there. You have choice. So does everyone else. You can influence people and circumstances, but you cannot shoulder in and pull the lever for someone else.

This seems like as good a time as any to look at one of the basic concepts of the New Age—"creating your own reality." I think it is a very misunderstood and misused concept. If you look at the laws of physics, you can see the basis of the premise. Energy attracts like energy. So if you are in a state of self-love you will attract things that will add to that sense of yourself. Likewise, if you are in a victim mode, you will attract those people and circumstances that will be only too happy to victimize you. That is reality.

But creating your own reality is metaphysical jargon for control. When you have a fear of the unknown, which is what life is, you will go to great lengths to make a control issue look like enlightenment.

In the name of creating your own reality I have heard all sorts of dangerous things. When someone dies—oh, pardon me, I mean when someone leaves the planet—it is because they "choose" to do so. I guess that means if they chose to, I can choose *not* to. And with this attitude, circumstance and biology have nothing to do with it. Does this sound like a helplessly impractical attempt at control?

This principle is shared by Science of Mind, *A Course in Miracles,* and lots of other simplistic systems. It is based on magical thinking. Magical thinking is something a child does. A child believes in his or her thoughts; she "is" a dolphin, he "is" a prince. Children "make" their parents like them. They think that if, in their childhood rage and fear, they wish an abusive father dead, and he dies, that they killed him. Children do not know the limits of their thoughts. Their worlds center around their reality. And so it goes for the New Age groupie.

People who feel powerless are drawn to the idea. The spiritual jargon gives them a false sense of control. People with AIDS are attracted to the concept, and why not? They figure, if they are powerful enough to create AIDS (were they?), then they must be powerful enough to uncreate it. But all they will create is a sense of failure, because when they work at creating their health and can't, they are left with an enormous sense that they have done something wrong.

On a very deep level, the level at which we are spiritually connected to the universe, it is true that we do create our own reality. I think, however, that we laypersons do not always possess the technology to make this useful information. I want to refer once more to the work of Deepak Chopra. He states that our reality is a perception of our sensory experiences and a belief in matter. These perceptions create limitations in our thinking. By shifting our perceptions it is possible to transcend these beliefs and to shift our reality. It is possible to shift our worldview collectively. In this collective way, as in an individual way, we can create our own reality, but it takes more than platitudes that are used to disguise reality. It takes work, risk, and clarity.

What *is* possible to do, and what is *not* spiritually damaging, is to say what you want in the universe. That way you do put out the energy to attract what you need. It also keeps you on track. Now, sometimes you'll get it and sometimes you won't. If you do, that is wonderful. If you don't, it doesn't mean you've failed at creating your reality, or didn't really want it, or any of the other list of "reasons" the true believers will give you. It just might be that it was an idea whose time was wrong, or there was a greater plan at work than yours.

The fear of being misunderstood, manipulated, or hurt often puts you in the space of needing to control. Control comes from a mind space, not a heart space or space of spirit. Spirit trusts. It is hard to unlearn the need to control. I think the first step is to acknowledge that while control may have become a technique for survival, it is an illusion at best. It doesn't work. The next step is to look at your life and identify the things you've tried to control.

A good place to start looking is where you feel the greatest pain. As you look at the things in your life that have caused pain, I think you will discover how much your urge to control things becomes evident. Your growing awareness can begin the process of choosing to let go of that urge—learning to relax. It can begin small and it can bring great joy.

I remember the first time I saw a bumper sticker with the word *powerless* on it. I remember thinking that I felt sorry for the powerless, out-of-control person behind the wheel of the car in front of me, and I puffed up with my own arrogance and control, which I mistook for power. Later, in a twelve-step program, I discovered that admitting that I was indeed powerless over my addictions—one of which was my need to control—helped me begin to reclaim my personal power. What I had been trying to do was control everything and everyone and manage circumstances that were beyond my control.

Surrender and acceptance are the antitheses of control and resistance. In surrender there is *trust*. It takes trust to surrender. Trust is a tough one for many of use to grab hold of since it is taken away from us very early by the denial, abuse, and broken promises that surround us as we grow up. When your feelings and thoughts and perceptions are disavowed, you cannot trust. You do not trust others and you do not trust yourself. Though you may look outside yourself for the answers, you expect to be abandoned, fooled, or disappointed. It is the natural extension of your childhood into the adult world. You trust your parents implicitly and are rudely awakened. You trust what they tell you in school only to discover that they lied and colored history to match their point of view. You trust God and then are told about a God who wants to control you. You cannot trust your instincts because they don't make sense in the real world of behavior. You replace trust with control or its counter-cousin, victimhood.

How do you begin to rebuild your trust? The first step is to know that you have lost it and see what remains that you do trust. There are some very basic things that you do depend on. You trust that when you call TIME on the telephone a recorded voice will give you the actual, accurate time. It is a small thing, but it is a beginning. You may even know that you can trust certain people to be untrustworthy. You can trust that some people will break agreements with regularity.

These are not the kinds of things that you are looking to hang your faith on, but they are real beginnings. In your journal, you can begin to list the things you trust and can count on. You'll be surprised at how many there are. You trust that the sun will come up every morning and that the days will come and go, each in its turn. You can also see that such things are not within your control, they just happen. There is a flow to the universe. Once you understand that the most you have ever had is the illusion of control, it is safer to let go; you can flow with it.

The universe sends us signals all the time. If events don't manifest the way you want them to, it doesn't mean that you aren't powerful. It means you cannot be a willful child all the time. If what you are creating is part of the universal flow, you will be a part of the river, trusting yourself to move downstream.

From Denial to Present Reality

I have a feeling everyone else could see that I was in serious trouble. Somehow I was so convinced that all I was doing with those pills and cocktails was relaxing that I failed to see that my life was falling apart. The mind can play amazing tricks. I could even explain away a blackout. And a hangover, well, it was always the beginning of the flu or something like that. I guess I need to be grateful to my friends, who finally couldn't stand back and watch anymore, for waking me up to the unpleasant truth.

Carolyn Blake, *Dover, 1990*

SAY THERE IS A DEAD RAT IN YOUR HOUSE AND YOU DON'T LIKE RATS. You are afraid of them and have heard all sorts of stories about how they carry disease and you can't bear to look at it. You just don't want to deal with it, so you pretend it isn't there. Every time you pass it or come back into your home you have to pretend again. You come and go as if there is nothing rotting away in your home. After all, if you do not acknowledge it, it won't exist.

You give a dinner party and don't mention the rat, so your guests don't either. After all, they wouldn't want to embarrass you. People don't tread easily on other people's denial. Your guests eat little and politely make excuses to leave early. Your denial is left intact. In your reality there is no rat.

Then your neighbors, unaware that you are so delicate on the subject, show up to complain about the stench and the flies. You are suddenly faced with that which you could have faced from the beginning, though now you are exhausted from the energy put into the pretense. If you had acknowledged the rat and your upset about it, you could have faced both the situation and your feelings and just removed the thing, leaving you with a clean house and a clear mind.

I tell this simpleminded story because what I am saying is simple but sometimes hard to hear. The truth is the truth! Denying the presence of a thing will not make it disappear; in fact, it adds energy to it. I suspect that if I asked you to, you could actually list all of the things that you deny. It isn't that you don't really know the truth, it's just that you don't want to know that you know.

"The truth shall set you free." That phrase may have gotten so stale through overuse that we fail to see its practical and simple wisdom. And yet the truth seems so hard to tell.

Denial is a pattern that you establish in childhood. Without denial you might not have been able to survive childhood. Without denial you could not keep childhood issues so present in your adult lives, but in order to master the present, you have to triumph over the patterns of denial.

Incest is often such a deeply invasive and painful experience that it may be cloaked in the veil of amnesia or denial for a very long time. Regardless of the depth of the denial, the effect on the life of the victim as both child and adult is all-pervasive. The secrecy and fear that attend incest become determining factors in all other relationships, and the denial stunts growth for years or forever.

Roxy told her story in a workshop. "I have three brothers. They are all older than I am. At some point when I was real little, I'm not sure exactly when 'cause I've blocked out a lot of it, they sort of started using my body. They just assumed that they could do whatever they wanted to me. So here I am, this little kid having sex and being threatened with brutality if I tell. I didn't even understand what was going on. How could I? I didn't know that sex existed. It was a subject that never came up and clearly was something that 'bad' people did. Quite a setup, huh?"

When a child is violated by another child, as Roxy was, it is because there are huge unmet needs being expressed by the perpetrator. And for the nonparticipating parent not to recognize reality takes an enormous amount of family denial and a deep unwillingness to see what is happening in the household.

In Roxy's case, her father died when she was young and her oldest brother became the man of the house. Along with a responsibility that he was not equipped to handle, he took on the role of all-powerful male, including his power over Roxy. He became a role model of manhood for his two brothers, who merely followed closely in his footsteps. Roxy could never tell her mother about the cruelty that she experienced; her mother, who needed to live with the illusion that everything was all right and who was dealing with her own fear and pain, couldn't see what was going on in her own home. In fact, in order to keep the family together, she needed to be blind.

The sexual, physical, and emotional invasion of the act of incest is deeply damaging, but the silence that always shrouds such events is just as damaging. To live in constant fear, with a dark secret, is to be cut off from childhood and deprived of the innocent joy of exploring life. In Roxy's case, the shroud of silence is still at work. Though her brothers will admit that it happened, none of them will talk about it or face the impact it has had on her life. Luckily, Roxy has achieved a great deal of clarity about her experience.

It's so hard to pierce through denial because it is a mechanism through which many of us have survived our childhood and its aftermath. As a child, if you knew that you were at risk every moment from an abusive alcoholic who was out of control, you would have freaked out. Your denial keeps you thinking that there is something you can do to change your behavior so that the abuse will stop. Your denial gives you the illusion that you have some control.

Denial is sometimes necessary to get through tough times. Many Holocaust survivors say that only by keeping up a wall between themselves and reality could they get through the most absolute horror. If they had looked at the horror and what was happening to others around them, their fear would have been all-consuming.

My friend Anna Shaller had cancer. Her doctor told her all the possibilities and what her chances of survival were. When she had finally absorbed the information and the fear, she asked him how she might go on living with the knowledge that she had only a slim chance to recover. He suggested that she confront the reality of her situation, look the fear and possibility of death in the eye, get her affairs in order, and then go into denial. It was denial after the fact, however, not instead of the fact. This kind of selective denial may be appropriate, but most people are not able to be selective. Denial becomes a way of dealing with life that is carried over from childhood survival. It becomes one of the tools of childhood that haunts and stunts adult-hood.

By now you know you were raised on fear and denial, and so you have little practice at telling "your" truth, or acknowledging that it would be safe or useful to say what you see, feel, and know.

Before you can begin to tell the truth, you need to be willing to see it, willing to go through the stuff that the truth brings up. Some of it is painful. But however good you've gotten at obscuring your own truths through substance use, power trips, or relationships, you need to dig hard and bravely to get at what is essential and true in you.

The New Age offers another way to obscure and deny reality that is at least as effective as booze and dope—that if you don't think about something, you won't make it real: by "creating" your own reality, you will keep it at bay. If, for example, you pretend you have no problems in a relationship, then there won't be any problems. If you do not like what you are thinking, just change your thoughts. If you don't touch the lump in your breast or think about it, it will not be there. This is all magical thinking. Denial is an adult version of magical thinking.

The real bitch of it is that the truth as we have come to know it exists whether you acknowledge it or not. Reality is reality whether you name it or not. Let me say that when I talk about reality I am talking about the collective reality that we live in because of our perception of matter and experience. It is important that we know it is possible to move beyond this confined way of thinking and living, but it is also important to acknowledge that what we know may not yet be useful in our day-to-day existence. We can work on rethinking the way the world works while living in it. It is too easy to skip directly to the principles of new science or the New Age without doing the work.

A Course in Miracles, the book allegedly channeled from God to an unsuspecting Jewish therapist, offers a version of magical thinking that skips the science: anything but love is an illusion. It states that the only reality is that of God, and that since God only created love, the rest is our illusion. When we live in our day-to-day world, we are in the illusion of ego, which in the course becomes pretty synonymous with evil. Again, the scientific reality is that matter is an illusion, but since I am currently living in the illusion of matter I need to honor that reality.

I remember in college wrestling with these concepts over bottles of wine in smoke-filled dorm rooms. Is life real or is it illusion? Ultimately, I decided, the question is bullshit. I was living in this physical reality (or "illusion" of physical reality) and so I'd better work it as if it were real. The chair that I am sitting on may be an illusion, but it is keeping my illusion of an ass off the ground. Does this principle of the course mean that if I don't acknowledge the chair it won't be there?

Even if your anger is an illusion, famine is an illusion, prejudice is an illusion, illness is an illusion, war is an illusion, and in fact anything but love is an illusion, this illusion is the reality within which we are spending this illusion of time. It is important to remember that we have finite minds and limited spiritual technology. Thus the information of infinity may not be useful. Can we use it in our daily lives without damaging ourselves and activating denial? Is it more damaging than nurturing? It is important to remember that it is possible to use the course or any other popular philosophy to avoid being responsible for hunger, famine, war, homophobia, illness, or your personal drama.

Does this principle of the course mean that if I like something and call it love, it is real? If I call an obsession for someone love, is it? If I say that my denial is an act of love, is it? If I declare AIDS is a lack of love, does that make it an illusion? I think not. Not in the framework of the finite experience. But I have watched many New Age junkies embrace this philosophy like a new designer drug and try to deny their way through life or AIDS or both.

They decided that if they didn't empower the virus (in English, that means if they didn't pay attention to it or let themselves even consider the possibility that it was there), it could not be in their bodies. With this trick many people managed to deny the existence of the virus until they became really ill, developed full-blown AIDS, and became victims of their own denial. Because they had not looked at reality, they were unable to put themselves into some kind of prophylactic, antiviral, or holistic program that would have extended and empowered their lives. The virus doesn't care if you name it, acknowledge it, or call it loving names. For many people the virus was present before there was a name for it and before they had given their power away to their new way of coping. If it's there, it's there!

Surely your attitude toward HIV is extremely important in terms of how you deal with it, but naming it doesn't empower it, and pretending it isn't there gives your power away to it. *You give your power away to anything that you deny,* though the New Age would give you permission for denial.

In a church in Los Angeles an aging immortalist guru type who is the creator of many pricey trainings stood in front of a group of church members, half of whom had HIV, some of whom were actually accompanied by poles to hold their intravenous medication, and told them that to believe in death is to allow it to happen. She even went as far as to tell them that those who believed in death and physical mortality were doing the work of the Antichrist. If you don't believe in death, you don't have to die. Given that quite a number of those in attendance were well on their way to their "transition," this was a fairly unconscious thing for an enlightened being to say. It seems that this woman has turned her fear of death into a dogmatic and judgmental philosophy. She had embraced new scientific thinking without compassion to further her own needs and fears.

Three cheers for new forms of denial! What you have done is use enlightenment in the way you can use drugs and alcohol—to avoid feeling, to avoid reality. Like a mind-altering drug, New Age denial will work for a while, but ultimately, in order to achieve true recovery and self-love, you will have to confront the issues that you find uncomfortable and be willing to address them in the deepest part of your being. An enlightenment junkie can avoid life for a long time, but not forever.

There are those who will come right out and tell you that emotional discomfort is not metaphysically appropriate. But discomfort can be valuable. It can tell you what needs to be attended to in your life. Sometimes reality causes upset. So there are a lot of enlightenment aspirers who think that upsetting or "negative" thoughts should not be allowed. They will go as far as to say it is not good for you to read the newspaper or have a confrontation. But life is full of confrontations; they can be growing experiences. The news, upsetting though it may be, is your connection to the world at large. This kind of confrontation with truth and reality allows you to contribute powerfully to the world in which you live. If you are not to be victimized by circumstances, you must at least know what they are, so that you can have choice and speak out about the things that move you.

Avoiding reality or denying the truth for the sake of complacency is irresponsible. In certain New Age systems, if a negative thought comes up, you're supposed to replace it quickly with a pleasant thought or affirmation to change the thought pattern. Well, what do you think happens to the thought you didn't like? It gets suppressed, it festers. It goes inside to support your personal belief system, slathered with metaphysical mayonnaise in an attempt to create an illusion. Mary Poppins as psychology!

That which you resist persists anyway (simple physics, simple truth!), so why not just treat your thoughts and feelings as an expression of what you think or feel in the moment? Thoughts and feelings are not a threat; they are just there to be looked at and learned from. The only way to change a reality you don't like is to face it and then get creative. Truth, like commitment and action, is one of the tools of growth and health. Denial, in personal life and New Age systems, is a tool of the core addiction.

Beyond denial issues there is another aspect of reality we need to explore. That is the difference between reality and our thoughts and feelings about it. Reality versus interpretation.

Did you see *The Gods Must Be Crazy?* A pilot flying over the bush throws a Coke bottle out of the plane. It hits an aboriginal in the head and eventually changes the nature of his civilization. The villagers think that since it fell from the sky, it must have come from God. The function of an object is up to the user, not the object. They had no experience of soft drinks, bottle glass, or airplanes, for that matter. They could only interpret the experience through their history. We do that too, all of the time. The truth is, the bottle never changed. Its reality remained constant. A thing is what it is, remember?

So you see, interpretation, perception, and reality often lead separate lives. You often attribute your emotional response to the object itself. You may see a bunch of beautiful flowers. In reality they are just flowers. You think or feel that they are beautiful. The aroma of the flowers may excite and intoxicate you, yet it may panic an asthmatic. If they look like the flowers on a loved one's grave, they may bring on waves of sadness and a flood of memories. If they are reminiscent of your wedding bouquet and the marriage was made in heaven, you'll love them. If the marriage was a disaster, you may want to tear them to shreds, stem by stem and bloom by bloom. None of this has anything to do with the flowers. The flowers have no point of view about themselves.

Not so with people. It is very hard just to see who someone is without filtering that person's reality through your own need, history, and interpretation. Similarly, it's hard to see your own reality. Your histories are built on a series of real events and yet their essential realness is obscured by your interpretation of those events. Your interpretation is usually based in the thoughts and feelings surrounding those events.

As you live in the present, each moment is colored by your history, your projections onto events. Reality lives in the moment, but you hardly ever live there. You become so attached to the past or fear about the future that it colors each moment. You replace reality with thoughts and feelings about it. Now, these are real thoughts and real feelings and need to be honored and dealt with as such.

You can begin to do this on a daily basis right here and now. When something happens and you begin to feel stress, or panic, or whatever feels discordant in your body, stop for a moment and do an on-the-spot assessment. Then, when you have time, you can sit down and go over the event to separate your thoughts and feelings and projections from essential reality itself.

You can use what you have learned in the Corridor and Breaking Patterns visualizations, which were about some of the ways that you have been led to misinterpret your history and your response to that misinterpretation, to guide you to how those events and patterns appear in your present reality.

Hooks to the Past

I've been so smart all of my life that I've always been able to manipulate my instincts into behaving.

Cristofer Shihar, *Los Angeles, 1987*

THE MIND IS ADEPT AT PLAYING THE GAME OF KEEPING YOU HOOKED TO YOUR PAST. The mind is the best tool that you have for keeping your dysfunctional system in place. Like a computer, the mind records input and can retrieve this input at any time, but unlike a computer, reprogramming it is harder. The mind has a mind of its own; it will retrieve information and run it through you without your even knowing. The mind makes sure that every time you nurture your Genuine Self, there is something to sabotage it.

After my divorce, I was living in a big New York loft with my children, a roommate, and a new Mr. Right. My roommate and some friends were doing a weekend seminar. They came home about four in the morning very excited and wanting to "share" what they had undergone. They woke my son and me, hauled us into the living room, and insisted that we name our minds. "Name our minds?" I queried. "How do you do that?" They told us to sit quietly and listen to our thoughts, to really pay attention to what they were saying.

I did as I was told, too tired to resist. Soon I heard a voice inside me saying, "This is ridiculous! What are you doing up at this hour? Your life is out of control. You won't be able to make it on your own. You need someone to take care of you. You aren't really happy. . . . If you were sane you'd be in a nice house and sound asleep. You shouldn't be hanging out with these people! Your friends are crazy and they aren't a good influence on your children! New York is no place to raise children. You should be back where you belong. . . . You should get married again. . . . It's too hard to be an artist. . . ."

"I've got it! " I shouted. "My mind is named Adele! " Adele is my mother. My mind had even spoken to me in her voice. I didn't know I held those thoughts. I didn't have a clue that undermining my bid for a new life, for freedom, and for creativity there was a running monologue making my very life feel wrong. New life, same tape!

My past, my upbringing, my parents' disappointed expectations—all of them were there, nagging for attention, keeping me from following my own path and breaking the rules of the system. I didn't realize at the time that among the things I was addicted to were those thoughts and the feelings they kept stirring up inside me. That's the drama addiction in a nutshell.

The mind is also capable of obsessive thinking and all of its offshoots, such as resentment and projection. If you are obsessing, resenting, or projecting, there is an illusion that you are connected to the object of these feelings and have some control. Obsessive thinking offers the illusion of control and that what you are thinking about is related to reality.

Resentment is an obsessive and projective kind of thinking. You pore over what you'd like to happen to "them" with your insides churning and your feelings running riot. Meanwhile, "they" are out there having a life, oblivious to your obsession, while thoughts of them are controlling you. Someone in a twelve-step meeting said recently, "Resentment is like swallowing poison and waiting for the other person to die." Enough said.

Obsession, projection (obsessing about what might happen), and resentment are not terminal. They are manifestations of the Impostor playing with your mind and they are treatable. You can begin with a written exercise:

First of all, choose something or someone that you resent or obsess about. Take a clean sheet of paper and begin by writing down your thoughts. Just pour out what is on your mind. Dump it all. No one will see this. After you have written down all the things that you have been thinking about the object of your obsession, projection, or resentment, skip a few lines and write down what you are feeling. Breathe through your body and let those feelings come up. What are you feeling? Do you feel hurt, abandoned, or betrayed? Are you feeling as if you don't matter or are powerless? You may have what appear to be conflicting feelings. That's fine.

Feelings don't have to make sense. Just keep breathing through your body and get into those feelings. Write them down until they are all out. Give yourself time to reflect on when in your childhood you felt like this. What is the relationship to your present and to other events in your life? See if you can spot a pattern.

Skip some more lines or grab another piece of paper and write down what happened during the events that brought about these feelings. Just the facts. What were the events and participation of individuals that led to this particular obsessive thought cycle? Just simple, clear facts. (I said and then they did . . . I wanted . . . here is what I got and did . . .) Once the story is reported and told, give yourself some time to reflect on the familiarity of the scenario. Is this the first time you've done this routine, or is it familiar—a pattern, maybe? When else have you been in this situation?

Skip some more lines and write down what you have been blaming others for. Where were you responsible in the matter? It is crucial that you not blame or load all of the substance on another. It is crucial that you not blame yourself. Get clear about your part; that's all you can do.

Once you are clear, write down how you wish things were. Get all of those hopes and regrets and lost pictures down. Let yourself feel the loss as you let these things flow.

When this is complete, write down the way it really is now in the moment—the way you need to accept it. Breathe through your body and be with your feelings about reality. Look and see if there is anything that can *really* be done to change the situation. If so, what would you have to do? If there is something that can be done, then do it. You can only break the obsessive cycle by being in reality, not your thoughts. If there is nothing to be done it is crucial that you understand that. Let the full impact of that fact hit you. Breathe through your body. Let your body feel the impact. This is the beginning of acceptance.

Now reread all that you have written. As you do so, breathe deeply into your feelings. It may be necessary to grieve and cry or rage in order to let go. It may take time to let go. Close your eyes and let yourself feel whatever is going on until you get some release. If none comes, sit down with these pages later. Examine your resistance to letting go. If you let go you would feel better. You might even feel really good about yourself. If that happened you'd be breaking the pact with your personal drama. Obsessive thinking is a tool of the Impostor. It wouldn't hurt you to ask some higher power or inner guidance for help.

When you have released your feelings, put the papers aside. If the thoughts come back, be aware of them and grab those papers to read through them. When you are clear that you have released this obsessive cycle, you may want to burn the papers as a symbolic way of letting go.

Sometimes the mind pretends to be feelings. When you are born you come with a full range of natural emotions. These emotions—love, anger, joy, fear, sadness, and their variations—are the natural parents of conscience. Conscience is a result of natural feeling and a healthy socialization process. When you cross your own natural boundary of integrity or compassion, your conscience and what you learned in a healthy socialization process will let you know. When you cross another's rules and come up against the system, guilt rocks you.

Responsibility is a function of conscience. Blame is not. It comes from guilt. You will need to blame someone, even yourself, if you feel guilt. When you inhabit a clearer reality, you act in accordance with your conscience. You naturally support and nurture others. You know that you are responsible for your feelings and actions and are accountable for them. It comes naturally.

Your connection to your natural conscience will be all that you need in order to follow the path of conscience. You don't need your parents or your religion or another system to tell you what is so. You don't need to be shamed into right action. As children you were taught to feel guilty by a system that needs you to stay within its limits. As adults you can be made to feel guilty easily, and you no longer need the help of others to do so. You might feel guilty for too much success, or too little. You might feel guilty for eating too much, or thinking a lascivious thought, or wanting things for yourself.

The most powerful tool of religion is guilt. If people can be guilt-ridden, they will not question a system that moralizes for its own purposes. Guilt is used to get you to do everything from giving to charity to allowing yourself or others to be abused.

Give yourself some quiet time to think about it. How much of your life is run by guilt? Look into your life. What makes you feel guilty? If you can name the things that you feel guilt over and can identify the source of that guilt, you will shift your experience of life. Who *told* you that stuff, and what did they have to gain by selling you a bill of goods?

Humiliation is a close cousin of guilt. You are generally humiliated when you do something that crosses someone else's limits and he or she lets you know in public. The response lets you know that your behavior is bad, or that you are stupid, inappropriate, or otherwise not all right. Humiliation is the external version of guilt.

If you experience humiliation and are embarrassed in public, you will begin to weigh your natural behavior against your fear of humiliation. You don't want to risk feeling like a fool. Tom was in the school play. His whole family turned out. His big scene came and he appeared onstage to say his lines. He opened his mouth and nothing came out. He tried and tried but couldn't get the terror out of his throat, and he involuntarily burst into tears. Finally the words came tumbling out. He left the stage mortified. When his family came to get him afterward his father teased him in front of his friends and called him Actor. The kids called him Actor from that day on, humiliating him with the memory of the experience. It is not hard to surmise that it took years before Tom was willing to risk speaking out.

You want to be acceptable, even at the cost of your aliveness and spontaneity. Again, take some quiet time to look over your life and explore what the fear of humiliation has kept you from doing in your life. What might your life look like if you did not hold back? Who has humiliated you in the past? Let yourself relive those experiences so that you can let them go and not be stopped by them. It keys into your shame. It adds evidence.

Shame, like guilt and humiliation, is learned. Guilt and humiliation are about what you do, but shame is about who you *are* when who you are is not all right with you. Shame can become part of your core belief about who you are, and it can be the foundation of many of your actions. Shame becomes the well from which springs your sense of self and the world.

Chemical dependence and compulsive behavior become a cover for feelings of shame. When you feel shame, you seek relief. If the relief is abusive to your life, it will eventually lead you right back to your shame—for the real addiction is to your shame and your personal drama that surrounds it. Your recovery can only begin when you are willing to delve into the shame and work through it.

People have told me their shame about feeling stupid, shame about having a foreign accent, shame about their sexuality, shame about their parents, shame about their failed expectations. People with AIDS can feel shame about their behavior or sexuality.

Internalized homophobia is another source of this shame. Of course homophobia in a homosexual is self-loathing. It is almost inevitable to have shame around your sexuality, given the way, as a child, you were introduced, or not introduced, to the concept of sex. Add to that the shame and confusion that same-sex attraction can produce in a child, and the depth of the scarring can be thick.

When producer/director Michael Bennett contracted AIDS he went into seclusion and denial. He withdrew from his friends and announced that he had a heart condition. I sat for many hours, many evenings, with his friend and mine, Ron Field (choreographer of *Cabaret,* director and choreographer of *Applause* and many other works), talking about how sad we were that Michael had felt such shame that he couldn't have the comfort of those who cared around him. We also knew that if he came out about his condition, it would be a major opening for others to feel free to say that they too had been infected with HIV. When Michael died he left a trail of people feeling incomplete because they were unable to see him, comfort him, or communicate with him before he died. Ron said that if he ever contracted AIDS, the first thing he would do would be to tell the press, and then do a show about it, so that his experience would be an inspiration to others.

What followed Ron's eventual diagnosis was quite different. He did just what Michael had done. He went into denial, never said that he had AIDS, and very few of us were ever able to spend valuable time with him before his death. Ron's deep sense of shame won out. Rather than follow his heart, he followed his shame.

Shame and guilt are some of the building blocks of the Impostor. This sense of self is so deeply implanted that it becomes your identity. You are no longer a person who makes mistakes, you *are* a mistake. You do not have to live in shame forever. Shame belongs to your Impostor, so as you embrace your Genuine Self, shame fades away.

Communication and Honesty

Not being a mind reader, I had a little trouble with the relationship I was in. Since he never told me what he wanted and I never told him what I wanted, we'd always do everything wrong. I think what I really did wrong was play the game. It never got either of us anywhere.

Diana Nova, *Santa Fe, 1990*

ONE OF THE MOST POTENT WAYS TO KEEP MALFUNCTION FUNCTIONING IS THROUGH YOUR COMMUNICATION. To attain Mastery in the present, you have to communicate in a way that enriches life, increases the possibility of intimacy, and tells the truth.

Until your malfunctioning communication patterns are lifted, the way you talk to other people and to yourself not only furthers the agenda of your Impostor but directly reflects your own dysfunctional behavior system.

Look at the way you most likely communicate with yourself. You probably have developed a habit of saying things to yourself that are not very nice, and possibly abusive. You adopt all of the self-deprecating, humiliating words that came your way and undermined your self-worth in the first place. If you spoke to other people the way you speak to yourself, they would probably want to slug you! If you called other people stupid as often as you say it to yourself, they would either begin to feel stupid or fight back.

Often you repeat the harsh, warping words of your childhood and absorb them. Circumstances trigger feelings that remind you of the past, and you attack yourself. You may have left the dysfunctional home of your childhood but brought its deprecation with you. The more you call yourself stupid, or fat, or slow, or mean, the more you will exacerbate the feelings, and so on. It is a vicious addictive circle designed to keep the Impostor alive.

Stephen Levine, a Buddhist Therapist author of many powerful books on living and dying, such as *Who Dies,* and a great inspiration to me, points out that when you stub your toe the first thing you usually do is swear at it, and be angry with it. Anger is not a very kind thing to communicate to your own pain. What your toe needs is some compassion—the same compassion that you need to communicate to yourself. The Impostor wants you to communicate with yourself in an abusive manner. How often do you put yourself down? The negativity that I hear people use with regard to themselves is very painful to listen to. I can imagine what goes on in their silent dialogue. These words are not the truth about your Genuine Self. It is important to listen to what you say, so that you can begin to see where the truth lies.

There is also the matter of communicating with others. We have become so guarded in our growing up that clear, truthful communication is difficult. If you spent a day carefully listening to your communication and seeing what part of it was edited, filtered, or designed to get a specific result, you would begin to see that your communication is as dysfunctional as the childhood that trained you to speak. But when you learn to say what you mean, you can begin to create the things you want and the responses you want. It means an end to manipulation and circumvention. All that is left is the truth. Your truth.

Whenever you tell anything but the truth, and do not tell yourself the truth, you are reflecting some aspect of your Impostor. Here's what I mean: say you are in a relationship with someone who abuses you. If you are afraid to address the abuse between you, it is most likely that you are afraid of losing the person, are afraid of being alone, afraid you will be abused more. The level of communication and its effect in your life depends on your accountability. If you go into denial and say that the other person is really good, that there is something that you did to create the anger, and that you'll be beaten if there is a confrontation, then you are a victim. If, on the other hand, you say to yourself that you are afraid you'll lose the person, afraid to be on your own, afraid you will be abused more, and have *decided* that you are not willing to run the risk of communicating your truth, you are being accountable. There is a vast difference, and telling yourself the truth may put you on the road to risking truthful communication with the other person.

Many gay men and lesbians are faced with the dilemma of the closet. I have heard numerous people testify to being victimized by society, stating that if they come out, their families will desert them, disinherit them, they will lose their jobs and have friends turn against them. The say that people fear, hate, and attack gays and so they can't come out. This is true for many people who are well known in the entertainment industry. They blame the industry. They fear exposure because the public is so ignorant and the people they work for are so homophobic. This puts them in the position of victim. They have given their power and freedom away to society, their families, their work.

A more empowering solution is simply to look at the way the world is and say that you are unwilling to face the ramifications of coming out. That you are willing to trade your full self-expression for feeling safe and letting your life go on undisturbed. When you make a conscious decision and communicate the truth to yourself and those close to you, when you stop making excuses for your behavior, you are accountable.

The truth will show up eventually, and taking responsibility for your communication with yourself may be the first step in telling the truth to others. My friend and colleague Rob Eichberg wrote a book called *Coming Out: An Act of Love.* By the end of the book it is clear to the reader that open, honest communication, though it may be painful, is an act of love, not just for the people you share your truth with, but for you as well.

When you communicate honestly and want to be heard, it is important that you let go of the results. Often when you communicate it is with the hope of controlling the outcome of the communication. This will just naturally inhibit what you say. Controlling what someone thinks or does after you talk with them is not your job. Your job is to communicate the best you can, hope to influence that person, and let go of the need to have it work out the way you want.

When you tell someone how you feel and what the truth is for you, it will allow you to really *be* with that person. Even if it's risky, it can free you. Say you are having a romance with someone and want more. You want commitment. Saying what you want would probably be the last thing you would think to do. You would most likely try to figure out what the other person wants, try to become indispensable, manipulate feelings, pretend things are cool the way they are. You'll do anything but ask for what you want. What if you ask and get a *no* in response? It might be worth the risk to know from the get-go that you can't have what you want. That way you can make some clear choices and will not have to pay the price of adjusting yourself and your communication to fit the needs of another.

Let's say that one of your friends does things that drive you crazy. You will tell other people about it. You may try to steer your friend away from the behavior. You will even spend less time in your friend's company and not enjoy it as much as you could. You'll do anything but say directly what you think. What if he won't like you if you tell him? What if she won't remain your friend?

You may need to have your friend hear you out. If the purpose of the communication is to control the outcome, you are lost. If it is to influence, you may be able to do that. If it is simply to be heard, you are in the winner's circle. If you are truly mastering your communication, you won't need to defend yourself—though of course you want to support your point of view—and you won't need to go on the attack, because attack wouldn't reflect your self-love or caring for your friend. But what if your friend *does* dump you? What if he or she doesn't see it your way? You may have to agree not to agree. You may have to suffer the consequences. You can't be responsible for your friend's reactions or response. You can be responsible for the way you communicate. Is direct, caring communication worth the risk? At least you won't have a lie between you. At least when you ask for what you want, you have a chance of getting it.

There are two areas of responsibility in communication: simply put, they are talking and listening. There are ways in which both can be done with satisfaction. The purpose of communication is to communicate, to speak, to be heard, and to hear. Truthful, vulnerable, spontaneous communication is powerful. You do not have to attach too much dysfunctional significance to your words, their outcome, or the words of others. Your sense of who you are should not depend on how you will be received, or if you will be liked, accepted, or agreed with.

This doesn't mean that you will not have your feelings hurt from time to time or will never find that your words have hurt someone else. Just because we know that what someone says is only his or her point of view, it doesn't mean that we are going to like that point of view. Again, the important thing is that you communicate truth in as supportive a manner as possible, and that no matter how a communication is delivered to you, that you not let your worth or your own communication be dictated by it. The important thing is that you communicate freely, responsibly, and clearly.

Being present in the moment is a significant factor in effective communication. It is hard to be with someone if you are really in your mind planning the result of the conversation while you talk. It is equally difficult to hear what someone is saying to you if you are retracing the steps of your morning, trying to remember if you turned off the coffeepot. On the receiving end it is most important that you learn to listen. When you find yourself judging, you are not quite present. Just notice the judgment and take care to hear what is being said without filtering it through your judgment. Just let the words travel through your body. Notice how they affect you. It's not necessary to pay close attention to the effect to be aware of it. You'll find it necessary to pay attention to the person talking in order to really listen and be able to enter into meaningful dialogue.

Know that what is being communicated to you are merely perceptions, feelings, and thoughts. That person's "truth" is just his or her truth, just as your truth is only *your* truth. Someone else's words may or may not be based in reality, just as yours may or may not.

There are many other components to communication. Noticing the body language and breathing of the person who is communicating may put you more in touch. If it looks as if you are not being understood you might ask if you are being clear. You need to be clear to be heard accurately. You may also need to agree on the terms you are using. In a workshop on relationships a woman kept saying to her husband, "All I want is for you to take care of me." He would respond that he couldn't do that. She would become more and more upset as their exchange went on. She kept saying, "Look, it's not a lot. I just want to be taken care of." He would go rigid. "I said I can't do that!" And so the exchange continued.

Finally I asked her what she meant by being taken care of. She said that it meant that her feelings be considered, that he treat her lovingly and care how she felt, that he spend time with her the way her parents never did. His response was, "I can do that." When she said that she needed to be taken care of, he was drawn to childhood feelings that were related to having to sacrifice his childhood to caring for a sick mother. He heard his wife ask to be awakened in the morning, brought breakfast, taken to the toilet, and so on. They were in different conversations, really. They were out of touch with each other.

Staying in touch with your own feelings will put you more in touch with yourself. If you are aware of what is going on in your own body, you will know if you are communicating fully, truthfully, and responsibly. It is also important to have compassion for yourself when all of the things you know about communication fly out the window. At least you'll understand the results. Here are the basics of communication:

Talking

- Stay in the present moment and with the person you are talking to.
- Tell the truth. Say what you mean, mean what you say. Say it all.
- Be accountable for choosing what you are communicating.
- Release your need to defend, attack, or be right. Be willing just to be heard.
- Know that what you think, feel, observe, and perceive are only your thoughts, observations, and perceptions. They may only be real for you!
- Be clear and ask if you are being understood.

Listening

- Be in the moment rather than somewhere else or planning your response.
- Just listen. Allow communications to go through your body.
- Know that what is being communicated to you are merely the speaker's perceptions, feelings, and thoughts. They may be real for her or him.
- Really hear and see the person you are communicating with. Notice if you are fully understanding. Notice breathing and body language.

It is wonderful to have this set of guidelines for communication, but what if your needs can't be met by following them? Sometimes you will find that what you need to communicate would be so hurtful, or would make so much trouble for you, that you decide to hold your tongue. You have too much stored-up energy on what you want to say to communicate with any clarity or safety. What do you do when you want to say what you feel even if you know it isn't true? What if you know you are responsible for your life but just want to be un-transformed and irresponsible for a moment? What if you miss blame?

I came home completely unglued one day and said to the man I lived with, "I feel totally inept. I feel like a failure, like my work is reaching deaf ears and it doesn't matter anyway. I have nothing left to say! I never had anything worthwhile to say, anyway! I feel hopeless!" He launched into a defense of my ability and wonderfulness. He said, "Hon, look at all the lives you touch. You are right out there where . . ." I know all that. And knowing had nothing to do with how I felt. I just wanted someone to hear my feelings, hear that I was hurting, not fix it! He was trying and I respect that, but I didn't need help, I only needed to be heard.

I now have a communication partner. A dumping partner. I can call my friend Ted Karavidas anytime and tell him what's going on, what's on my mind, what I'm feeling. We have a deal. I can dump all of my insecurities, fears, and garbage, and it's his job to just listen. I do the same for him. Do you know how hard it is to find someone who will just listen—be willing to hear you, not want to give you a dose of reality, make you feel better, fix you?

When we communicate we put ourselves in a position to move out of the darkness into the light. When we communicate we move from survival to life. As we become more skilled at communicating we become less afraid of the truth and less afraid of the results of our communication. We use words to enrich our lives, to risk growth, and to allow ourselves to become more intimate with others and ourselves.

Mastering the Illusion

Mastering the Illusion

I thought I'd changed my life. I thought that I really loved myself, but it wasn't real. Notice I'm here in this workshop! I'm trying one more time to find out who I really am. I thought I had it, but I was fooled. I know who I'm not but that's not the same thing. I look different, I talk different lingo, I dress differently. I thought that I felt different, but I don't really.

John Ferrin, *Los Angeles, 1990*

As you come out of the trenches of childhood and begin to walk on the ground of your present, you will get some sense that the battle to be your Genuine Self is won. This is exactly the point where so many people begin to relax their guard. As you work on yourself, you may feel sure that you are on the right track. Surely you have your recovery in hand and are on the way to Mastery, leaving behind your dysfunctional self, your dysfunctional childhood patterns, and your drama addiction. But your recovery may be an illusion. The Impostor can still lurk, ready to ambush your Genuine Self.

You may develop a false sense of well-being. You may have embraced ways to find self-love and recovery that look and often feel good, but those methods could eventually lead you back to the dysfunctional systems you thought you had shed. It is possible to spend a lifetime in the illusion that the path you are on will lead you to the promised land, if only you do it right. The look may be different but the result will be yet another entanglement with the way it's always been. This is what I call *dysfunctional recovery.*

Dysfunctional recovery occurs when you free yourself from the traps you have lived in—and then fall into fresh traps. You may think you have left the past behind, but it may just be wearing a new disguise. It may be wearing the cloak of recovery and yet you may be using your recovery as a shield against the issues that still keep you from your own authenticity. It may be disguised as a Master, come to lead you into the light, who may in fact lead you to your self-loathing. It may come in the guise of a new career that seems to have come because you have embraced your self-worth when in fact it is a substitute for self-worth. Dysfunctional recovery is a master of impersonation.

You may think you've gotten your life together, and yet you feel apart from your Genuine Self. If you are still out of harmony with yourself, you are still somewhere in the addictive process. You may have changed your life enormously, changed your behavior, your friends, your thought patterns, and your diet. You may have handled chemical dependency, changed the way you talk about yourself, embraced a sense of God, and done good deeds—but if you still feel the way you always did about yourself, if you are still making yourself wrong and trying to be better, you are still locked into the system. You are still prisoner of your need for mere survival and addicted to your history. And history will repeat itself until it's outlived its usefulness.

In this section we will explore some of the illusions that fool you into thinking that you've achieved Mastery. We will explore what happens when you give up your old dysfunctional life yet still can't quite define who you are. Exchanging one rigid system for another as you seek spiritual renewal, you may fail to realize that all you may be doing is trading systems, trading parent figures, trading oppressors, and trading the activators of your childhood feelings for a new set of activators. The system through which you seek spiritual growth may replace earlier dysfunctional systems and be equally dangerous for you.

In this part of *Life Mastery,* I'll offer you some exercises and processes with which you can check out your recovery and determine if it is nourishing and nurturing or if it is dysfunctional. Once the light of truth shines on your new behavior and beliefs, you can begin to recover your Genuine Self, and solidify your recovery and your Mastery.

Trying to Define Yourself

There was always some dark shadow hanging over me. It spread itself out between me and my sense of who I am. The light is just beginning to dawn through all of those gray areas. I have always been told a lot about who I was expected to be and I think that has kept me from knowing and surely from loving who I am. I am learning, though. I learn more and more every day. And I'm learning fast! What if all I've got left is tomorrow? If so, I want to spend it as myself, not as someone I made up to please other people.

Tony Head, *Washington, D.C., 1988*

WHEN WE EXILE THE IMPOSTOR, THE ILLUSION OF FREEDOM CASTS ITS SHADOW OVER US. We don't have much practice at being our Genuine Selves. No one has given us a blueprint for how to sustain that kind of authenticity. Some people may try to give you rules for discovering yourself, but there are no rules. Discovery has no rules.

When you begin to exercise your new freedom, you may assume a different false identity; you may allow yourself to be defined by a new system. That's part of the recovery process and there is no wrong in it. You aren't the way you were, but you aren't in touch with who you *are*, either. Like an alcoholic who has given up drinking but retains the behavior patterns of alcoholism, you may be a dry drunk.

When I got a divorce, I assumed that I would assume my true identity. At a loss for a new role, I embraced feminism. I thought that if I burned my bra and refused to be treated like a sex object, I'd find a new, independent self. But I was secretly longing to be treated like a sex object! At the very least, I needed to be sexual.

What I was defining as "finding myself" was in reality resistance to male domination. I became sexist, tough, and generally took on a lot of the characteristics that I hated in men. I became butch, all decked out in combat clothes and cowboy boots. One day I was approaching a bank of elevators in a high rise where I had been doing some construction work and as I glanced up I caught sight of what I thought was a cute guy. As I approached this cute guy, much to my horror, I discovered that it was my own reflection! (Well, at least I thought I was cute!) So I went to a lingerie shop and recommitted to the satin and lace that I loved. Keeping what I needed from feminism, I began to reembrace my femininity in all its contradictions, allowing my own style to emerge. It was a step. I was a long way from finding an expression of my Genuine Self, but I was closer.

In counseling I worked with a man who told me at our first session that he was a landscape architect. It was what he had always wanted to be. Ever since he was a child he had his hands in dirt. He helped his mom with her garden, and as a child he loved to create order and to see things grow. When it came time to leave childish things behind, he went to college and got a degree in business. He went into the family firm at graduation. In school he became a drug addict and alcoholic. He struggled through two divorces.

He went into treatment, got clean and sober, and set out on the path to self-awareness. He decided to leave the family business and pursue his suppressed desire to be a landscaper. Everything in his life was looking good. He was doing what he had always wanted, he worked his twelve-step programs and did service there, he had reconnected with his second wife, and he was successful. But deep down, he wasn't happy. Deep down, something was wrong. What we finally unearthed was that while he was following his childhood dream, it was just that, a childhood dream. It was no longer what he wanted. What he wanted to do now was drug and alcohol counseling. While he hadn't been playing life by his family's rules anymore, he wasn't winning the game.

As you enter recovery, not only can you often redefine yourself into another mistaken identity or way of life, but you may continue to subtly take your sense of self-worth from outside yourself. One of the things that always struck me about some of the most powerful and successful people that I know is their inability to "really" enjoy their power, talent, and success.

Michael Bennett created *A Chorus Line,* and changed the face of the theater. He was responsible for *Dreamgirls* and *Ballroom* and on and on. His genius left its mark on an endless array of theater classics. In his apartment overlooking Central Park was a testament to his agile and brilliant talent. In one corner of a mirrored coffee table, reflected in a mirrored ceiling, sat an arrangement of Tony awards. At least nine, as I recall. But Michael was a possessed and restless man. His appetites were insatiable and no one could fill his need for love and self-worth. No number of Tony awards, hit shows, accolades, or the huge amount of influence and money that he had earned ever put out the hunger for self-love. His search for "enough" was relentless. Yet this talented, brilliant man never found what he longed for. He could not erase, nor would he look at, the pain he experienced over who he thought he was.

If you find that you still look outside yourself to define yourself, to get your worth, as though it were to be gotten from anywhere but the self, watch out. There isn't enough anything—not food, drugs, praise, or love outside us—to give us ourselves.

While I was still working around the theater and seeking some evidence of who I was, I underwent a little demonstration of my own need for external validation. I was lucky that it came early enough in my evolution as a teacher to keep me from damaging anyone with my need. I had created a cadre of followers and acolytes who thought that I was a source for their theatrical creativity. They "needed" me, and unbeknownst to me, I needed to be needed. I counseled and worked with famous people and hopefuls. I had a whole persona created around the mystique of my work. I was successful and loved, and lived in the illusion that all was well, but still, I didn't feel satisfied. No matter how much I was needed, or how powerful a presence I created, I couldn't seem to get satisfied. Then I went to see the film *The Rose.* There is a scene where Bette Midler comes staggering out into a stadium filled with screaming, cheering fans. The screen is completely filled with them, maybe a hundred thousand! I had an uncontrolled thought that spoke loudly in my head: "Maybe that would be enough!" I was shocked! Then, just as quickly, I knew there was no such thing as enough. At first I felt very sad, and then I felt relieved. If there was no such thing as enough then I could stop looking. It just isn't out there. It isn't available! I can't "get" enough. I am enough. No illusion can fill such a need.

As you seek to sustain your Genuine Self, you bring with you some very powerful habits from childhood that trick you until the alarm goes off. Listen for the wake-up call. If you keep too busy, or don't allow that you may have fallen into a few traps, your denial will create a new veil through which you can filter your life.

It is important to stay in touch with your feelings about your life in the present. They will let you know where you might be fooling yourself. Your feelings can guide you to the dysfunction that you may still be living in. Remember, you are dealing with a powerful system that has had you hooked into it for a very long time. It is not going to let go so easily.

Dysfunctional Systems = Dysfunctional Recovery

I was going to two meetings a day. I had so many books on my bedside table that I couldn't find room to put down a glass of water. I didn't know if I should read A Course in Miracles, Codependent No More, Out of the Shadows, or Creative Visualization. I've chucked most of it. Compulsive is as compulsive does.

Daniel Adams, *Los Angeles, 1987*

WHEN MOST OF US WANT TO RECOVER OR BECOME ENLIGHTENED, WE GO TO SOME SYSTEM OR OTHER TO FIND OUT WHO WE ARE. Instead, we find out who we ought to be. The job of this book is to smash systems of all kinds that bind you to the past, give you the illusion of growth, and serve your personal drama and core addiction.

As I've discussed before, therapy, encounter groups, alternative spirituality, metaphysical mind control, and pop philosophies all have systems that you are constantly trying to conform to, with leaders you are constantly trying to please. You replace your dysfunctional family with dysfunctional recovery. Your recovery then perpetuates this unseen addiction.

This core addiction is the reason you only recover to a point. The Impostor can fool you into thinking you've found the answer, the thing that will bring you back to your Genuine Self. Tricky as always, the Impostor gives you a new system that you can cling to instead of seeing reality. It will keep you seeking the answers from without when you know they are within. It will make without look like it's within. And so you embrace malfunctioning systems in order to recover from dysfunction. The recovery is an illusion. In this way you re-create and perpetuate the system that warped you in the first place.

You may look to your guru, therapists, or program to tell you how to do it. This will leave the responsibility for your recovery outside yourself. If you were really aware of the system you labor under, would you let someone stand before you and a roomful of people and tell you how to think and feel, just the way Mommy did? If you didn't need to feed the system, would you adopt a new system to set your limits and define what is right and wrong? The system is hungry. It wants you to keep on feeding it, and it will feed you with enough freedom to explore but always to come back for more.

The Impostor will let you go to meetings, to forums, to symposiums and workshops and keep throwing information at you so that you can endlessly be a student in the process of learning about yourself. You can become process junkies! If you aren't your awful former self, then you become your "getting better" self. You'll do anything, believe anything, to keep from becoming your Genuine Self. You'll do anything, that is, but think for yourself. You will allow the illusion that you have found yourself but you will not become yourself.

Twelve-step programs offer you a powerful chance at recovery, but even though there is no guru to give your power away to, nor a rigid formula to follow, your Impostor can trick you. Your Impostor wants you to stay in the program—not to recover, but simply to be in a recovery program. The system wants you to keep trying to get better, because if you are still trying to get better, the system is safe. If you are trying to get better, it means that you still don't know who you are, and the system lives on.

I'm not saying that the twelve steps don't work; I know they do. I work them. They are lifesaving! In fact, I think that the twelve steps of the program, if really lived, could bring us all, including the dysfunctional society and government within which we operate, to health. I see people go into the program as a place to hide from their reality. They misuse the principles and language of the program while their lives stay entrapped, allowing the Impostor to flourish in the illusion of recovery.

I coached a singer named Linda who fit this description. Linda had given up her career in favor of booze and drugs. She went into a recovery program and had abused no substances for two years. She said that she was ready to have her life back—and that included having a hot singing and songwriting career. She spoke a lot about honesty and being responsible. She talked the talk of the program, but in her personal life she manipulated the man she was in a relationship with, and used her sexuality as a tool to entice people to help her until she had gotten what she wanted. Though she had developed her own powerful style of singing and writing, she was ultimately unable to do the emotional work in her life and performing that she would have needed to be more than just ordinary. She had an extraordinary talent, but the Impostor was smart. It led her to think that she was out there in the risk zone where brilliance and creativity live. But in fact, it was only the appearance of risk.

Her life had been spent looking good, and so she knew how her recovery should look. She knew how her life should look. She thought she knew how her singing should sound and so was afraid to risk being out on the emotional limb it takes to be great. She was afraid to let her life fall apart and not look good. Her recovery and her career are in the same place, and her fear has led her to that place where there is no risk of moving beyond the Impostor into a sense of her Genuine Self.

One of the offshoots of the twelve-step programs is the inner-child syndrome. There are many teachers out there who want you to pay them a lot of money to put you in touch with your inner child. I think this can be a little dangerous. One of the things that happens for those not ready for real recovery is that they get a new set of "reasons" not to be responsible, not to be adult. Much of this work leaves its followers in emotional childhood, trying to get little Larry or Lorette's needs met. I hear grown men in my workshops say things like "Little Jeffrey isn't ready to talk about that yet." Well, Jeffrey, you aren't little anymore and it may be time to face the uncomfortable task of being a grown-up.

The inner-child syndrome allows adult children to wallow in their unresolved past and have an excuse for being childish. John Bradshaw has done some powerful work around childhood issues, but I must admit it sets my teeth a bit on edge to see him ride onto a stage on a tricycle. While I acknowledge that I have many unresolved childhood issues within me, the little girl that I was is long gone. I am an adult with unresolved childhood issues. I am a full-grown woman with many childlike feelings and needs. I can't give little Sally what she didn't get.

But I *can* look at my childhood, see what it was that I needed, and begin to release the past and get what I need in the present.

If you are going to do inner-child work, please do it as an adult and be treated like an adult by your teachers. If you are talked to as if you are children, you are feeding a teacher's need to be the adult and keep you needing him or her. Children are dependent. There are those who want you to depend on them.

With many systems of traditional therapy, your personality and needs will immediately be consigned to a category, at the expense of your uniqueness. What the systems of traditional therapy don't recognize is the presence of a core addiction to personal drama and self-loathing. And you can swiftly return to that core addiction, this time using therapy as an activator. There is no therapeutic category under which to file core addiction, and therefore it doesn't exist.

Most traditional therapies do not deal with the addictive process and the grip of codependence at all; such things are written off as pop psychology, self-help. After all, to recognize that this addiction exists would mean that the therapists themselves would have to acknowledge and confront their own codependence—their own needs to be needed and have the answers. The therapist will continue to live in his or her system and will therefore have a very rough time guiding you through yours. All they can do is support the illusion of progress. Please understand that I am not talking about all therapists. I have had some wonderful experiences in therapy and think that no matter how much you read, learn, pray, and discover through other means, the personal approach that therapy provides is essential. Left to our own devices, we cannot sort out all that we are trying to master. It is the *rigidity* of many systems of therapy that can be damaging and keep us in our patterns from the past. Classically trained therapists tend to be reverent about their systems and so when faced with clients, see those clients as pieces to fit into an already existing mold. More attention is often paid to what those therapists think about their clients than to the clients themselves. Such practices never consider that a lack of progess might result from the systems of therapy. The therapist can show you how to fit into the system and thus give you the illusion that you are making progress, but illusion is not healing.

One of my friends is a therapist. She has loosened up greatly over the years, but for a while she was so system-bound that she could not see that any ideas from outside her counseling system were valid. She holds my work and the work of my colleagues as "less than" the work that she and her colleagues do. She said that it could not possibly have a deep effect because it does not follow the rigidity of her beliefs and schooling—although because many of our clients have AIDS, she sees the merit of a superficial, short-term solution.

In working with people who are facing their mortality, we are discovering just how deep the work can go. We also see how, faced with the urgency of possible death, people can accomplish a great deal in a short time. I know this isn't necessarily good news to the kind of psychoanalyst who wants you to come five days a week for an exorbitant amount of money and become a dependent.

Within the traditional model of therapy and psychoanalysis there is a designated patient or client/therapist role. These roles are rigidly defined. Many therapists are appalled by the idea of shifting this relationship. Some therapists actually live in fear of running into a client in the grocery store, as if their clients don't know they have to eat, like other humans. This attitude replaces boundaries with rules. One of the things that a client seeks most is a model for flexible boundaries.

Freudian psychoanalysis is a perfect system to perpetuate the self-loathing addiction because it centers all the responsibility on the child and his or her suppressed lascivious nature while negating the role the outside world plays in shaping or warping that child. Only original sin rivals this concept for original guilt.

Woody Allen is a great example of the limits of rigid psychoanalysis. He not only examined every aspect of his nature on the couch, but offered it up to the public in his films and writings. While all of his torment and investigation brought brilliance to celluloid, I can't say much for its effect on his life.

My own first experience with a traditional, rigid psychiatrist was a cross between enlightening and painful. It was enlightening because I moved past wallowing in misery and did some productive introspection. The work was painful partly because I had to look at some very unpleasant realities, but mostly because when the illusion of well-being wore off I realized that at the end of my therapy I would be normalized, trained to be the way I was brought up to be. It left my Genuine Self submerged, waiting to be discovered and nurtured.

Trust in Yourself—and Not the New Age

I*f I wanted to continue to feel guilty about my whole life,
I'd have stayed Catholic.*

Jimmie Schaeffer, *Los Angeles, 1986*

WHEN YOU ARE NOT READY TO TAKE THE RISK OF DISCOVERING YOUR
GENUINE SELF, YOU LOOK FOR PAT ANSWERS. You seek the promise of
peace at the cost of reality, and at the cost of your creativity and
uniqueness. It happens when you succumb to the system that warped
your childhood, when you surrender to the tenets of rigid therapy,
and also when you blindly embrace the systems of the New Age. Any
discipline or teacher who will tell you what to do robs you of your
journey and replicates the malfunctioning systems of family, school,
and religion in the name of light and love.

The New Age words are different, but the message is the same.
The message is that there is a right way to be and a wrong way. The
New Age religion can reinforce the idea that *you* are wrong, and not
the system. When some New Age guru tells you that you are a perfect
expression of God, you are told exactly how that expression must
manifest itself. There are rules and limits set on the way you should
think, feel, and speak. There are acceptable modes of dress, decorum,
and expression. All things that threaten or question the system are
denied or disavowed. Sound familiar? When you are in pain you will
grasp at straws as if they were strands of gold. These straws lead you
right back to the addiction, to the Impostor.

When my own life, as lived by the Impostor—who seemed unable
to do the job of wifing, parenting, being sober, or drawing a self-loving
breath—was so out of control, some force from my Genuine Self sent
me on a quest for wellness. After some time I became a tentative
follower of Muktenanda. Swami Muktenanda was an Indian guru who
lovingly guided people in the way of his line of Masters toward their
own relationship with God. I would go to South Fallsburg, New York,

to his ashram to be touched by his wisdom. My devotion was tentative because it is hard for an addict to get too spiritual. What I heard there was profound and egoless, but it took a long time for me to understand what I learned on a meaningful, visceral level. I got a new therapist, I got my divorce—and then I got ESTed.

The rules of the EST training and organization were completely rigid and controlling. Before I explore the problems with EST, I want to give the training credit for being the single thing that was able to penetrate the fog that surrounded my life and for bringing into clarity some powerful principles that have formed the fiber of my healing and work ever since. I also think Werner Erhardt was the first person to grab the attention of the Western world in a way that began to popularize enlightenment. It amazes me still that this all happened almost in spite of the system that he set up.

The leaders of EST condoned and engaged in abusive behavior. I sat in a room for two weekends and let the "trainers" call me an asshole, and yell at and demean and belittle people in the room in the name of "getting better." I allowed myself to be convinced that my resistance to this treatment was my resistance to life, my attachment to a picture of who I was. This may have been true, but abuse is abuse. In the EST elite, proper transformation looks a particular way, dresses in a particular way, and has a correct jargon and thought process. To be really enlightened, it has to look and sound just so.

People who abuse others are not transformed beings, no matter how much they can justify themselves. Those who are abusive are stuck deeply in the mire of their addiction to their personal belief systems, and if abuse is the core of that belief system, then in EST they have a perfect system to operate within. If your fundamental shame is deep enough, you'll need to control others in order to mask your vulnerability and lack of personal power. The best way to do that is to become part of a fascist elite. Once you have a system like this, no one will question your authority and rightness. If people do challenge you, then they are the villains, the fools, and they must be purged from the ranks and made wrong.

And so with EST I found myself smack-dab in the middle of a cycle of addiction, in a system run by system addicts.

It has occurred to me that Werner might have been the first person to discover codependence; rather than write about it so that others could recover from it, he built an organization on it. Guilt and manipulation and emotional abuse were the tools through which he put a huge network together. As in many a malfunctional family, it was all done "for your own good" through a veil of denial, and with "honor thy father no matter what" as the mantra.

For a while I tried to fit in, but when I tired of being mistreated I left. I went next to the Actors Institute, which was originally sort of an EST for actors. Dan Fauci, who founded the institute, attracted many creative people, and to be sure, there were those who came wanting to find a system to fit into. The problem for them, however, was that one of the bottom-line purposes of the work at the institute was to put people in touch with themselves as the source of their own creativity. Once you are in touch with your creativity and your uniqueness is honored, it is less likely that you will fit into a mold.

Thousands and thousands of us, myself included, have flocked to New Age seminars that promise to open the door to all that we desire, offering easy access to the spirit and rules about how a good and transformed person should behave and feel. Unlike EST, New Age spirituality may not be a jolting experience, but it still has a system for you to fit into. The New Age may make you feel good; but what you don't see is that feeling good, if it is a substitute for looking at reality, is just an illusion. It works just like substance abuse. You are in a new kind of denial, a cycle that tells you all is well even if it isn't. Your Western guru of choice will tell you how to be. Sound like orthodox religion? It is. It is New Age Fundamentalism.

What you are offered as a spiritual path is the false salvation of dogma. A system in a new disguise. But it makes sense that you look for someone or something to tell you what to do. It is what you have always done. First your parents, then school, then religion, then society. In this way you can maintain some level of irresponsibility for your own life. Though New Age systems tell you that you are totally responsible for your life and everything that happens to you, here lies the opportunity for the Impostor to grab hold of you and drag you back to childhood. Here's what I mean: if you are totally responsible for everything that happens in your life and you are still unable to be all-loving, all-compassionate, healthy, and financially abundant, then you must be doing something wrong. Though the system may say that responsibility does not mean praise, blame, or guilt, the opportunity for feeling like a failure who has brought it all on yourself is ever present. Failure produces guilt and feelings of unworthiness.

When a guru sets him- or herself up as the answer and the answers are all based on false promises and premises, that guru will disappoint you. In the West, we don't know how to be true gurus, we only know how to be public-relations stars. In the East, one becomes a guru by study, talk with God, contemplation, and earning the trust of one's spiritual teachers. Trained in humility and humanity, a guru walks humbly with God and his or her own guru. Respect is core. In the West it is more often than not about packaging and marketing. We are an instant-soup society. A good PR firm can sell you God in a way that is very hip.

In my first year of AIDS work, I led a workshop at Whole Life Expo and was also on a panel with others in the field. I took a tour of the convention area, where the wares of the New Age were being sold, with my friend Jimmie Schaeffer, who had an AIDS-related neuropathic condition and walked slowly with a cane. He said his body felt like a toothache all over; nonetheless, he wanted to see what all of this was about. After seeing the most expensive crystals on earth, cosmic facials, electronic ways to open your consciousness and raise your vibes, instant changelings, New Age foodstuffs—all for a pretty price—Jimmy began to laugh wildly and twirl his cane around his head. Through his laughter he said, "I have a feeling if Jesus Christ were here he'd be turnin' these tables over left and right!"

Stephen Levine and Ondrea Levine, his wife, partner, and a powerful spiritual vessel, were the first to point out to me the difference between genuine spirituality and the New Age. They are also people who live by the principles that they teach. What they teach comes out of years of listening to the wisdom of the people they help guide to their inner truths. They have discovered the humility of a deep inner connection with their spirituality and are thus able to touch you with your own heart and love. They are powerful guides and deeply committed human beings. They live their lives in the richness of service, mutual respect, and respect for the human condition.

Perhaps because the Impostor can't afford to be exposed and because the New Age is so good at deception, you can find quick, easy, safe answers. There was a time for me when therapy was really painful because I might connect the dots, see the real picture. Since I couldn't stand the discomfort, I left therapy (again!) and went to Louise Hay, who was then not yet very well known as a metaphysical healer. I was tired of feeling bad. I wanted to feel good. I left each session loving myself and filled with hope. But what I had done was trade real healing for an illusion. All of the reality that I had been overriding with "feeling good" showed up, and I nearly went under. It took years of distance and the advantage of hindsight to realize how dangerous it is to ignore reality. The Impostor feels safe if we learn some rhymes and songs to make us feel temporarily good about ourselves.

In order to maintain the illusion of well-being and avoid reality, it becomes necessary to keep things looking and sounding a certain way. The jargon and style of enlightenment can be substituted for real life. One Fourth of July in New Mexico I went to a party with my friend Franke. It was a party filled with New Age disciples and we were practically the only ones not dressed in white. After a few hours Franke casually mentioned that we probably should leave soon, as we were expected somewhere else. Suddenly all heads turned! All eyes cast furtive glances in our direction. "Should?" A chorus rang from the metaphysically correct crowd! *"Should?* There is no such thing as should!" ventured one on his own.

A *should* disguised as a platitude is still a *should!* I have always loved to wear black, but in the early years of my work in the spiritual community Louise Hay would tell me that it was a mourning color and not the right energy. The implication, I suppose, is that *I shouldn't* wear black and that I *should* wear colors that would be more appropriate. Never mind my personality and self-expression. Personally, I would rather look to *Vogue* magazine for fashion statements than *Whole Life Monthly*. What about spontaneity and creativity? Judgment disguised is still judgment. Rules disguised are still rules. All of this provides a perfect environment to fan the flames of our hidden addictions to "the way it's always been." Addiction is addiction. Telling people how they should be, whatever the disguise, is abusive. I'm happy to report that Louise now wears black and looks gorgeous in it.

Abuse is passed off in the name of God as in both organized religion and the New Age. I was struck by how abusive it was for Pat Robertson to tell his flock that God told him he would take him if they didn't give him eight million dollars. I am struck by the spiritual abuse implied when the preachers of the right condone homophobia and teach hatred in the name of God. I was equally struck by the spiritually abusive nature of two things that Marianne Williamson was quoted as saying in a *Los Angeles Times* article. Ms. Williamson calls *A Course in Miracles,* which she uses as her vehicle, "a complete system. It has no holes." This indicates that it is also a closed system. In a closed system there is no room for disagreement. If you follow the dogma you are right. If you stray you are wrong. The course and the name of God are used, as with the fundamentalists, to indicate that there is a direct line to God and you are not on it. When asked about reports that she is prone to temper tantrums she responded that "sometimes you have to be a bitch for God."

To justify abusive behavior in the name of a New Age God is the same sort of behavior that put the fear of God into so many children and drove a wedge between them and their spirits. To justify abuse in the name of God comes from the same system that condoned the Crusades and claimed the right to put a price on the head of Salman Rushdie. God does not give certain needy people the right to be abusive or to work out their unresolved childhood issues on you.

Spiritual leaders, old and New Age, need to be responsible to the principles they teach and to those who would turn to them. If they tell people to live in a way that they can't, then they are once again replacing the dysfunction of childhood with an equally dangerous substitute. None of us can live exemplary lives. We are human and in that humanity there is grace. I have been known to be a bitch on occasion myself, but not in the name of God. When I'm a bitch it's because I forget God.

The important thing on the road to recovery is to regain your own personal power. You cannot find your personal power by quoting the course, or Marianne, or me, or Louise, or John Bradshaw. The important thing is, what do you say? What do you think? What do you know? Or have you given your thoughts and feelings away to yet another demanding parent? Have you cast your lot behind another ego that needs you to need it, another leader that needs to be "the one"?

Brilliant teachers are the ones who empower their students to find their own way, not slavishly follow the teacher. If you need your teacher, you have not been taught well.

When you can see the relationship between your addiction and the new systems that you have swallowed, you can acknowledge the system, and begin to move past it, to release it. There are brilliant teachings within many of these disciplines, religions, and programs that are available. The problem lies not with the information, but with the mode of delivery, which allows "disciples" to adopt any system wholesale, or canonize any teacher.

If you can think for yourself and allow your intuition to draw you toward the light, then you can take what you need from the potpourri of spiritual offerings that lie before you. When you are willing to think for yourself and feel deeply, you can discover what will nourish and nurture your Genuine Self. You can take the things that resonate for you and let the pundits preach to those who are not ready to be powerful, loving, and aware of their self-worth. You will no longer need to worship a system or pontificator, to idealize or starmake. You will no longer be satisfied with the illusion of well-being and you will no longer let anyone offer you the illusion that you need them in order to love yourself. *You* know what you need.

Challenging the Impostor

Now, let me get this straight. You want me to let go of everything that has kept me going all these years? You're crazy, lady. You are one crazy broad!

Herman Alvarez (Diva), *Los Angeles, 1986*

WHEN YOU ARE WILLING TO FACE REALITY AND SET ASIDE DENIAL AND RESISTANCE—WHEN YOU ARE WILLING TO STOP TRYING TO CONTROL EVERYTHING—YOU WILL BE FACED WITH A BASIC TRUTH. Here is the truth that you've been most resistant to: you are wonderful, loving, and powerful. You deserve to have a wonderful life and to be loved.

This truth doesn't sound like something you'd spend a lifetime both seeking and avoiding, but still it totally blows your cover. If you own up to being all right, to possessing a Genuine Self, then the Impostor is through. If you recognize yourself, the system you have been living within is exposed and can't serve you anymore.

Since this Impostor has been so good at living your life for you, you begin to think it is who you are. As you have discovered, you have survived by "being" the Impostor, so giving up the Impostor quite naturally enough feels like facing death. In reality your life is on the brink of beginning. Life and "survival behavior" cannot occupy the same space.

Your survival has depended for its survival (so to speak) on your fear that you would have nothing if you let it go. The Impostor has constantly fooled you into thinking you are who it is. It is going to fight to stay in there. It will do almost anything, as you have seen, from promising you that things will get better, to telling you things *are* better, to letting you think it's gone, to wooing you with a thousand promises and lies. Let's keep in mind that what you are dealing with is an addictive cycle. It wants everything to be the way it's always been and sometimes your personal drama will make a last valiant attempt at breaking your hold on reality. Remember, sabotage is a familiar tool of the Impostor.

Not long ago I began working with a singer as a performance coach. For years everyone had told this woman how she should perform. Well-meaning people had tried to fit her into some preexisting format. It didn't work. What worked was to free her to sing and express herself the way she had always wanted to. So she had a lot of emotional work to do, not to mention the task of shaping her material. Very rapidly she shed years of other people's ideas, and tons of emotional baggage, including a deep sense that she would never make it. Her work became free, clear, totally her own.

Her commitment and action and willingness to press through the discomfort and explore her dark side brought light and passion to her singing and courage to her songs. Out of this commitment, opportunities and people to support her began to show up. Everything was going smoothly and suddenly she began to choke. Literally choke. Her throat would begin to close up. She had let go of so much of the Impostor that it actually had her by the throat and was hanging on for dear life.

If she and all of us are to keep the saboteur at bay, we must be vigilant. You need to look at the fact that not only are you giving up the things that have stood in your way, but you are also giving up the tools that allowed you to survive childhood and adolescence. You are giving up an entire way of life. There is—appropriately, I think—some sadness as well as fear around the loss of the way it was.

You also experience a certain loss and sadness at the passing of a phase of life, the passing from dark to light, the passing from lie to truth, from survival to life. The sadness is the loss of a familiar friend that served you well for a time. There is genuine grief to be experienced and honored. You may resist the casting away of that which is familiar, has served, and no longer serves.

Yet you do not have a process for these passages.

We have a process to honor the death of friends and loved ones. We learn that there is life after those that we have depended on die or end a relationship. There is life after a job ends or a show closes. Yet we have no form for the grief that comes with change and growth. If you are going to make a move to release your Impostor and the entire sense of yourself that you have been living with, you need to grieve. You don't have to grieve for it all at once or for the entire concept. You may want to take time to grieve for each pattern as you let go of it, each habit that you replace with choice, each life rule as you break it. The point is to experience the loss so that you can move on. Part of the grieving process is to acknowledge how well-served you were by these survival techniques and the Impostor who acted them out. It is not that you have failed in some way, or even that they have failed you. They have simply outlived their usefulness. You will find more about this process in the "Mastering Emotions" section later in this book.

You also need to recognize that all along your Genuine Self has been tugging at you to be remembered. The very fact that you have survived indicates that your Genuine Self has been there all along, telling you that you deserve to feel good about who you are. It is the presence of your Genuine Self that has allowed you to attract the things that do work in your life. It is the real self that has brought the loving relationships, great jobs, and success you already have. I want to suggest a simple exercise that can help you to begin to see who you really are, to begin to recognize that you already are the person you strive to be.

Stand or sit in front of a mirror.
Just look at yourself for no less than five minutes.
Just look. No combing, no makeup, no shaving.
No affirmations or mirror work that comes from acting work or
    metaphysical discipline. No fixing at all.
Just be with yourself.

Breathe deeply through your body.
As you exhale, occasionally let out a sound.
Be very aware of your feelings.
Listen to your thoughts.
Be aware of any judgments or discomfort.
Just be aware.
There is no reason to correct or to make yourself wrong.
There is no wrong and no right way to do this.
All there is to do is to look at yourself.

Just be there with yourself and let whatever goes on, go on.
Look into your own eyes.
This is who you are.
You may linger longer than five minutes if you like.
You are getting to know your Genuine Self.

It's a very simple exercise. If you do this for at least five minutes a day it will help you to recognize yourself. You will come to recognize a person who is wonderful, powerful, deserving, and always present. *You already are the person you are striving to be,* because you are your own best role model. You have the grace and the power that you have yearned for, and it is high time that you allowed yourself the pleasure of your company—the full range of your ability and emotional life can express itself through you.

Mastering the Body

Mastering the Body

I have spent my entire life in some sort of contest with my body. When I was a kid I pushed it to extremes just to prove I could do stuff the other kids did and that I wasn't a sissy. As an adult I have pumped it and used it and tried to make it feel good with drugs. Now that I am sick I realize I have no control over it. It doesn't work the way it used to and it sure doesn't look the same. But somehow I like it better. It's just my body, the contest is over, and I'm at peace.

Michael Saunders, *Los Angeles, 1988*

MASTERING THE BODY IS ABOUT BEING AT PEACE WITH YOUR PHYSICAL SELF. Your body is the vehicle through which you can express who you are, and through which your spirit can express itself. It is as if you are given your body as a vehicle for your particular personality in this lifetime. Your body goes through your life experiences and memories. It is important for you to tap into its potential.

Because you identify yourself very strongly with your body, your physical self is a great place for the Impostor to act out.

Unless you are sick or injured, you probably only pay attention to how your body looks. You exercise it, you stuff it with food, you hate it, you love it. You drug it or pour alcohol into it. You feed it health foods and vitamins when you think it needs help. You rely on your body to get you through life and support your most compulsive behaviors and worst sleep habits—without paying attention to any of the signals that it may be sending you. Most likely you compare your body to the ideal sex object, the most desirable face and form promoted in the media, designed to make you hate the way you are and spend megabucks becoming something you're not and weren't intended to be. You tan it, you plastic surgery it, and you work it. Yet you pay little attention to its real needs.

Your body, however, has a mind of its own. Without your help its functions go on quite miraculously. Your heart beats, your blood flows, your immune system protects you, and your eyes tear. You hardly notice any of these natural wonders until your body malfunctions and your health is threatened.

In this section we will explore the relationship between state of mind and illness, between emotional well-being and physical well-being, between thought and healing. We will also discuss the fact that knowing all this and using appropriate techniques do not always work. There will always be those who will turn hope into denial, and failure to be physically cured into an opportunity for self-blame. I will offer no techniques for healing the body. What I will offer is a way to use illness or other conditions in your body as a rich source of information that can help you master your life. Your body, where everything is stored, has lots to reveal to you if you will listen to its signals and heed its guidance. Often, if you consult it, your body will gladly tell you what it needs.

I'm going to include addictions and recovery in this part of the book, because your body is where substance abuse is played out and where other types of compulsive and obsessive behavior and thought take a toll. When you are a practicing addict, the well-being of your body is usually the last thing that you are interested in or conscious of. In fact, with addiction, it is your mind that keeps you from hearing the messages your body is sending you. A major step toward recovery is developing an awareness of your body.

Mind-Body Connection

I have been picturing myself well for about a year now. My body has gone through quite a lot and I don't deny any of that reality, it's just that I think of myself as well and so I lead the life of a well person. The other thing is that I have a really powerful relationship with my body. When it tells me to sleep, I sleep. When it tells me I have an infection, I call the doctor. This way of living is new for me and quite profound. My body told me to quit my job and do something I love. What a trip!

Max Navarre, *New York, 1986*

THE FIRST TIME I EVER CONNECTED THE MIND AND BODY WAS WHEN A FRIEND OF MINE IN COLLEGE GOT AN ULCER. His doctor told him that he would have to eat white food, give up booze and spices, and go to a therapist. A therapist? Clearly this doctor was quite ahead of his time and certainly had the right idea. Ulcers are stress-inspired physical conditions. If my friend had just changed his diet and taken medication, he would have quelled the symptoms for a while, but the underlying cause of his malady would have remained.

By examining his life he could see that the drive to be a straight-A pre-law student and to live up to his family's expectations was stressing him out. This awareness offered him a couple of choices. He could either change his major, and pursue something less stressful and more of his own choosing, or he could change the way he thought and felt about the choice he had already made. He opted for the latter, but ultimately couldn't make the emotional and mental transition. A recurrence of pain convinced him to drop out of law and study languages, something that excited him but held no threat.

Back when I was seeing Louise Hay to "feel good," she introduced me to her booklet, *Metaphysical Causation of Illness.* In it was a listing of particular physical maladies and their relationships to their nonphysical cohorts. I found it fascinating and helpful. I began to look further into these relationships. In this material, which is now included in *You Can Heal Your Life,* she would state what personality or character trait had created the physical problem, and then offer an affirmation to heal the disease or condition. So if cancer is caused by deep-seated angers and old resentments, you can say an affirmation to let go of the resentment and (theoretically) the cancer. Though all of this seemed very simplistic it piqued my curiosity about the connections between physical and psychological health.

I pursued this connection without much urgency until suddenly my own home was invaded by illness. My son, then Stephen Fisher, now actor Fisher Stevens, had been having some pain in his joints and swelling in his glands. I took him to a bunch of doctors who looked for "mono" and found nothing, dismissing his symptoms as part of adolescence. I wasn't so sure. I had a nagging worry that I couldn't suppress.

We were living in New York and Fisher was due to go to Chicago to visit his father and my parents. I called a former family pediatrician in Chicago and set up an appointment. Because he wasn't feeling ill, Fisher was less than pleased to put down his catcher's mitt and go to the doctor. He was put through a series of tests and then released to go back to the baseball diamond. I spent some agonizing time waiting for the results. The doctor called me. My son had Hodgkin's disease.

It still amazes me that my entire world changed with a single piece of information. I was stunned and terrified. I walked around in a daze. I gazed out the window and saw people casually strolling down the street or hurrying to some appointment. I hated them for leading normal lives while I was at risk of losing my child. I wanted to shout at them, "How can you just go about your business while this is going on! "

After I gathered some loved ones around me and went through self-pity and Fisher-pity, I went into action. I set up an appointment at Sloan-Kettering with a pediatric oncologist. Next, I made an appointment with a nutritionist and a therapist; I called Louise Hay for some hope, a juju witch doctor for some magic, several church networks for prayers, and the airlines to arrange Fisher's flight home.

I waited at the arrival gate with a knot in my stomach. As passengers began to deplane I began to search for my handsome, bright, energetic kid. Suddenly I saw what looked like a little old man; it was Fisher hobbling off the plane, ashen, hunched over, looking frailer and shorter than I remembered. I was appropriately alarmed. What could have happened to him? Why was this kid, who only days ago had to be pulled from a ball game and stripped of his mitt to go to the doctor, now barely able to move?

Suddenly, with a flash of light, I saw the answer! He had been with his father and my parents. Not that this in itself could send one from childhood to senility, but what I assumed to be true was later verified: with the very best of intentions, they had been treating him like a cancer victim. A dying child. I could just see his father casting furtive glances as he sighed, "Save your energy, son. You'll need it to fight this thing. Go to bed now." I could just hear my parents as they waited on him hand and foot: "I'll do that, honey. You're sick. You don't want to strain yourself."

Though I am sure they were well-meaning, what they had done was to overwhelm him with their fear and their projections. They had begun to treat him as if he were dying, and now it looked as though his body barely had enough energy left to live. As he made his way slowly toward me, I began to chuckle.

After a long, tight hug and some tears, I said to him, "Do you know that you don't feel sick?"

"Mom, I have cancer!"

"Yes, I know, but do you know that you don't feel sick?"

More annoyed now, he said, "But I could die from this."

"I know, but do you know that you don't feel sick?"

"But, Mom . . ." Then he paused, and I could tell that he was beginning to pay attention to his body.

"Where do you feel sick?"

He began to look. He looked and looked but couldn't find a place. I saw him brighten and we began to laugh. My kid was back.

We went to Sloan-Kettering. As we waited between tests and doctors I began to think about the effect of his emotional state on his physical well-being. Later we went to Louise Hay. We went to lunch. Mindful of the mind-body connection, I asked him, without knowing exactly what I was after, to look at what he thought he might be able to get from having this disease. Right off the bat, he said, "Attention." He knew that in the drama surrounding his parents' divorce it would take something equally dramatic to get attention. I assured him he could have mine. I suggested that he make a list of the other things that he wanted. When the list was finished we could see which things were possible and if there wasn't some less life-threatening way to go about getting them.

He wanted to spend more time with me. That would be my pleasure. He wanted to inspire the other kids at school. That was up to him. He'd like his dad and me to get back together. Not a prayer. And so on, down a pretty long list.

This story has a very happy ending. A very long time later Fisher is alive and well and still inspiring people. I would be foolish to try to pin the reasons for his recovery on any single thing that he did. He gave up red meat; did yoga breathing; had his spleen removed; had radiation; was loved and supported by an enormous extended New York family; looked the truth in the eye; did Louise's tapes and affirmations as well as those of the Simontons, who were doing ground-breaking work with cancer; laughed a lot, as Norman Cousins suggested; was prayed for on several continents; and had a powerful medicine man on his side.

The reasons he is well are not important. What is important is that he was able to learn a lot of valuable life lessons from the experience and could create a very powerful relationship with his body that serves him to this day. Without the pain and the threat of death that he had endured, I too learned many life lessons from his experience. I also learned a lot about the connection between the mind and the body; I would put all that to use in the work that I would be called to do in the future.

Fisher's experience, along with the research that I did in the ensuing years, became a powerful tool in my work around the AIDS crisis. In the early days of the epidemic it seemed that people diagnosed with AIDS were given six months to live. That's what most of them did. When doctors began to observe some people breaking the rules, they tagged on an extra six months to the prognosis, and then six months more, and so on.

A New Age movement began to shape a different point of view about life after an AIDS diagnosis. Louise Hay was one of the first people to offer hope of survival to those told that they had an inevitably fatal disease. Those who followed her word gained strength and self-esteem. They thought they were healing their bodies of AIDS. In truth, all but a very few were experiencing an infection-free grace period that most often follows a first encounter with an opportunistic infection. They would have some healthy time and become sick again. Visualizations and affirmations alone cannot fight a powerful virus.

As Deepak Chopra has pointed out, we believe in illness. He calls the body a field of ideas and interpretations. We have certain perceptions and beliefs about the body and disease. We believe in disease and the process of aging. It is possible to change our personal and collective belief systems. Just as it is possible to shift your perception of who you are, it is possible to shift your perceptions about your physical body. Again though, I must warn that since most of us have not yet developed sophisticated technology to effect this change, we must approach health from what is ultimately possible as well as what is immediately possible.

The New Age approach to disease, or "dis-ease," as the New Agers like to call it, seemed to take the attitude that illness was always self-created, and thus could be uncreated. As I explored that idea, I decided that such an attitude supported denial, and left you feeling like a fool and a failure if you got sick and died. Platitudes are not enough to change years of thought patterns that support disease; with rare exceptions they can't cure carcinomas, viruses, and broken bones or AIDS. Nevertheless, there is something very powerful in the connection between attitude, personality, and health.

Giving credence to this mind-body connection but knowing that people needed more, I created the AIDS Mastery Workshop. Somewhere between denial and predictions of certain death lay a wide spectrum of options that can lead to a rich and full life. I believe that it is the mind that most helps to determine the quality of life, regardless of the physical circumstances.

In a study at Harvard, Dr. Herbert Benson proved that meditation reduces stress. Norman Cousins showed us that laughter can hasten the healing process. Surgeon, author, and lecturer Bernie Siegel, in *Love, Medicine and Miracles,* has pointed out that certain patients (he calls them "exceptional cancer patients"), who clean up the tangled resentments and relationships in their lives and participate vigorously in their course of treatment, have a better chance of recovering. The tricky part is that everyone is different. As Dr. Howard S. Friedman has pointed out in his recent book, *The Self-Healing Personality,* each of us has a personal mechanism that is unique. Some people beat the odds against a terminal condition. What allows that to happen? We don't know the precise answer to this yet, but there are people for whom mind over matter seems to be a working option.

Some years back I went with Tommy Tune, the magical performer and director/choreographer, to see Fisher perform in *Torch Song Trilogy* on Broadway. At dinner Tommy complained of a headache. By the time we got to the theater his head felt as if it were splitting. This occurred just as crystals were about to burst on the scene as a new phenomenon. Naturally, wanting to be metaphysically correct, I had one in my pocket. Not at all convinced that it had any healing properties, I gave it to Tommy, telling him to place it on his temple and to put his head down on his knees for a while.

I giggled with skepticism, but by the time the first act began, he was feeling better. By the time we went backstage to visit with Fisher and Harvey Fierstein, the play's brilliant star and author, the headache was completely gone. Tommy told me weeks later that he had been getting frequent headaches, but after the *Torch Song* incident he had not had any more. My skepticism wasn't the point. The point was that there was something in Tommy's belief system and personality that allowed his headache to go away. The process of healing the body is quite mysterious.

What is not so mysterious is the fact that the body has much to offer in the way of useful information. If you have a condition in your body, never mind how it got there or who is responsible for it, how can it become a useful tool for you? How can it contribute to your life? A tumor, a broken leg, or chronic anxiety each holds a wealth of useful information about how to treat the condition, as well as tons of information about your life. Well or ill, these conditions have messages for you. Your body has always had messages for you. Some are subtle. Some are not so subtle.

A simple example is a hangover. A hangover is a signal that you have abused your body. It is a clear message that your body cannot tolerate the poison that you have poured into it. It's not, as some have clearly misinterpreted, a signal to have a Bloody Mary!

Both physical and chronic emotional conditions (such as constant depression, stress, and anxiety) reflect issues in your lives. I know that when most people get sick they fight the illness or condition, but your body is not a battleground. If you fight the condition, it will fight for its life. If you fight the condition, you may miss the point.

If you are using some sort of visualization that does battle and it seems to be working, keep it up, but try this first. Pay attention to the condition. Let your body talk to you. You will be guided to a healing of the quality of your life and to Mastery of your body. In the following visualization that is just what I will ask you to do. Let your body talk to you. You will ask questions and let the answers flow from your body, not your mind. Here is the visualization:

Reconnect to the energies from the center of the earth
   and the infinite universe . . .
Let those energies vibrate in harmony with your own . . .
See the energy as light surrounding each cell . . .
Allow it to vibrate and to awaken the memory sleeping there . . .

Direct the energies to the condition in your body that
   most needs to be addressed.
Let the energy flow to the condition or an area that represents it.
Does it exist in one place?
Many places?
Continue to send energy there,
   to this condition that most pulls your attention.

How do you feel about yourself with this condition?
Let yourself feel the feelings related to this condition . . .
What feelings come up as you breathe through it?
Take your time . . .
Let out a sound . . .
Continue to be aware of how you feel about yourself and what
   emotions are related to this condition . . .

Ask the condition what it can tell you about your life.

What do you need to know?

To pay attention to?

What is the condition trying to tell you?

Listen to your body . . .

Let it talk to you . . .

Let your thoughts go and be with the condition.

Stay there as long as you like . . .

When you understand on a visceral level what it is that the condition has to tell you about your life, take some time to let the information in.

Just be with the information . . .

Is there anything else it wants you to know?

Take your time . . .

Next ask the condition what it is in your life that it wants you to release.

What does the condition want you to let go of?

What do you need to release?

Breathe through your body.

Let out a sound.

What do you need to release?

Listen to your body and the condition . . .

Spend all the time you need to . . .

When you have listened, just let the question go and be with the answer.

What feelings come up?

What would it be like to release those things or people?

See yourself free . . .

Take your time, and when you are complete, let the images and sensations go . . .

Now ask the condition what it is that you need to allow into your life.

Ask the condition to guide you to those things and people.
What do you need to embrace and to allow in?
Let the condition speak to you . . .
Listen to your body talk . . .
What do you need to allow into your life?
How do you feel about this information?
Breathe through your body and let out a sound.
Take all the time you want . . .
When you have the information that you need, release the images
  and feelings.

Once again be aware of the condition in your body.
Allow a mirror image of yourself to appear before you.
Be with yourself and breathe deeply.
How do you feel about yourself?
What do you see?
Look into your own eyes.
Let out a sound.

The condition you have trusted to guide you to information about
  your life can also be asked to help you treat it.
Ask it what it needs and then listen . . .
What would begin to ease this condition?
What would be useful in treating it?
Let the information flow . . .
Next ask how you can best live with this condition if it does not
  go away?
Let it tell you . . .
Let out a sound.
Be in touch with your feelings . . .
Ask the condition if it will be your guide and help you in the fu-
  ture to discover things about it and you.

> *When you feel that you have learned enough, begin to bring your*
> *awareness away from the condition and back to your entire*
> *body.*
> *When you are ready, bring your awareness back into your room.*
> *Open your eyes and be still for a few moments.*

This is a good time to write down what you have learned, what the condition has told you about your life, the things that it has guided you to let go of, and the things that it has suggested allowing into your life. This is also a good time to make the kind of list that Fisher did, about the things that the condition might bring into his life. That way you can begin to find nurturing and healthy ways to have those things.

There are many ways to support your physical health. Now is always a good time to begin to take care of yourself and to enjoy the richness of life around you. You may not be able to heal your body but you can maximize its well-being and live in harmony with it, thus experiencing the grace of Mastery.

Real Recovery

I'm glad I am clean and sober even though I have to deal with HIV. I figured if I am going to die, I want to be conscious for it. I also know that if I want to get things in order I will have to live without the things that create chaos. I've had to give up a lot of ego. They keep telling me to turn it over. That's what I keep doing. You do it, God. I don't know how!

Harry Endicott, *New York, 1990*

HARRY, LIKE MANY OTHERS THAT I'VE MET, FOUND THAT BEING IN RECOVERY WAS A NECESSARY ELEMENT OF DEALING WITH BEING **HIV-POSITIVE.** As he says, if there is to be completion and clarity, the things that created chaos and confusion must go. For addicts, that is whatever substances they use and the issues that created the addiction.

As an addict myself, I am amazed that I could go for so many years without seeing that the substances I was abusing were abusing my body. When we do drugs we damage our physical well-being. When we seek recovery, a major part of that recovery goes on in the body. Our bodies become accustomed to the physical response to the substance, to the physical relief as well as the emotional relief that the substance brings us. We also become used to the painful aftermath, not just in terms of the emotional shame but the physical discomfort or pain of coming down or getting too high.

Though the effects may appear more dramatic with alcohol and dope, the damage is just as devastating with food. Some eating disorders, such as anorexia (inability to eat, no appetite) and bulimia (binge-and-purge cycles), can lead to physical death. The fear of not being perfect can leave you thin and very ill.

As an overeater I always wished I had an eating disorder that would let me be thin. Without understanding how devastating anorexia could be, I wished that I would lose my appetite. I tried to become bulimic but I only mastered the binge part. I was one of those overeaters who could take off twenty pounds anytime I wanted to. The problem was that I could also put back twenty pounds and then some, anytime my Impostor wanted to.

I have always been an overeater. I ate when I was happy, sad, or bored. It was sort of a family trait. One of the few places I would ever really spend time with my father was when the two of us would sneak into the kitchen at night to steal food from the refrigerator. As I have grown up, I have faithfully kept my bargain with my childhood and used eating as a means of comfort and of self-deprecation. With typical addict thinking I always knew that I was going to handle it tomorrow. That this was the last pig-out. That my plan to be thin by the end of the month would go into effect the very next day, and the next and the next. And I teach this stuff!

When I began to do work with AIDS, I seemed to become oblivious to the pounds creeping onto my body. Not that I didn't watch them creep on. Like any self-respecting overeater, I weighed myself at least three times a day. But my concern for this rapidly compounding interest wasn't too great—not until I actually noticed that when I would mount the scale in hopes that I had lost weight and find that I had gained instead, there was a real deep sense of satisfaction. This panicked me. The Impostor had done it again. The Impostor was feeling happy just as I began to feel like a failure. The pounds that I was accumulating were keeping me safely from being as powerful as the rest of my life would indicate. The pounds that I was accumulating would keep me feeling like Daddy's little fat girl.

I went to a few Overeaters Anonymous meetings. There I discovered that the way to lose weight is to quit eating the things that make you fat. What a concept! It also occurred to me that if I lost one pound a week for the next year (as opposed to an immediate thirty-pound drop, which I could regain overnight), I would lose fifty-two pounds.

Progress was slow, and so I went to a Los Angeles doctor who designed a food plan to work with my life demands and to eliminate foods that are incompatible with my physical system. He said, "No pasta or bread or other starches." I said, "Oh God!" He said, "No sugar." I said, "No big deal!" He said, "No seafood for a while." I said, "Okay." We bargained for a diet cola now and then.

The most important thing about this food plan is that it is just that. A plan. It is not a rigid system. If I'm at a banquet and red meat is served, I can have it rather than create an issue or not eat. If I am at a dinner party and the menu is not on my plan, I may eat what is served, because part of the plan is to serve my lifestyle, not control it. Thus, rather than have to force my life to fit a rigid system, the way my childhood did, I can be guided to support my health and my well-being.

Soon all the feelings I had been eating to suppress came up. This is true whenever you give up a substance that you have abused. These feelings are in the body. They are there for you to examine and learn from. They are there to guide you to the childhood memories that created the discomfort that led you to the substance in the first place. When I first gave up cocaine, all of my feelings of not being smart enough shot right to the foreground. I remember saying to a friend, "Now I know why I did this stuff!" But at that point I hadn't a real clue why I actually did it. I did know that doing drugs was no longer an option for my physical health and that feeling the emotions that made me so uncomfortable was actually good for my health.

When you have a true desire to stop abusing your body with a substance—or if you are at bottom and the only other choice is oblivion or death—the process of recovery begins. Recovery is a very clear blending, balancing, and harmonizing among your body, mind, and spirit. Your relationship to each will change. I now have a completely different relationship with my body and my body has a close relationship with my spirit. I no longer let my mind talk me into doing drugs, alcohol, or allowing myself to be fat. My Impostor would love for me to be fat so that she could be front and center again. This does not seem like a viable option for my life. In recovery I have really gotten to know my Genuine Self. My body is much more in harmony with the essence of that Genuine Self.

Mastering Emotions

Mastering Emotions

*Y*ou mean I'm not going crazy? You mean these are
*just feelings? You mean people actually have this going on
all the time? Wow! I guess this is what I've been afraid of.
It's scary, but it's very alive!*

Terry Lopez, *Los Angeles, 1989*

BY NOW YOU KNOW THAT WHEN I SAY MASTERING THE EMOTIONS, I DON'T
MEAN CONTROLLING THEM. Mastery means that you will have your emotions, feel them, express them, and not have them run your life. You
will also not mistake your feelings for reality. Most of us spend a
lifetime suppressing or dramatizing our feelings. Like just about everything else, we learned this trick in childhood.

Before you encountered a system that told you to hold your feelings for an appropriate time, or that what you were feeling was wrong,
or that what you were feeling wasn't what you really felt, you were
an expressive little being. As I have already mentioned, but for
bodily functions, the only things babies can do is feel and express.
As you grew up and became socialized you learned that expressing some of your feelings infringes on what is going on in the world
around you. If you are guided well, you learn to have your feelings
and express them in a way that doesn't disrupt everyone else; you
will not become an adult version of a child screaming on an air-
plane.

For the most part, though, you learned about what is socially
appropriate to feel. More importantly, you learned to express yourself
by the rules of the systems you grew up in. You lost your spontaneity
and perhaps even your ability to know what it is that you feel. You
became afraid of feeling raw, of feeling too deeply, of letting your
feelings show. The same systems taught you to substitute learned
responses such as guilt, shame, and self-consciousness for feeling. We

fear being out of control, and yet we cannot really control our emotions. We can suppress them, but they won't go away.

Ron, a legislator in a midwestern state, took a workshop on childhood issues. He told a story about when he was very small and had saved up money to buy a super-triple-scoop ice-cream cone. His mother always said that one scoop was enough and that's what he always got. The day arrived when he counted out his coins and, lo and behold, there were enough! He felt proud. He was thrilled. His little body was shaking with anticipation and delight. He ran to tell his mom. She merely said it was no big deal and nothing to get so excited about, and she sent him off to school. He felt himself put a lid on his excitement, afraid to further dampen it by telling anyone else. After all, it wasn't anything to be excited about.

After school his excitement began to bubble up again. His mom took him to the store without the slightest bit of encouragement or congratulation. He went in, placed his order, handed over his cold, hard cash, and waited, trying to suppress the bubbling joy. The man gave him his cone. It was perfect. Just the way he had imagined it. He could no longer contain his excitement and rushed from the store. Then he tripped. The cone flipped from his hand and crashed to the sidewalk, destroyed. So was he. He dissolved into a stream of uncontrollable sobs. His mom came from the car and patted his head, assuring him that everything was all right. There was nothing to be upset about. It was only ice cream. There was no need to cry or make a scene. But Ron knew what he was feeling, even if his mother minimalized it and told him that his feelings were inappropriate. The problem is that when you are told often enough that your feelings are unnecessary, you begin to adjust. You will begin to make your emotions appropriate for the system.

Emotion is simply energy. It has a velocity and a density and it occupies space. In his book *The Family,* John Bradshaw refers to emotion as "*E*-motions. Energy in motion." All emotion is, is energy on the move. Emotions are not good or bad. They are not right or wrong. They are not positive or negative. They are just feelings powered by energy.

Your Impostor has adapted a mind-set that labels emotions positive or negative. To be sure, there are feelings that wrap you in a sense of well-being and others that are unsettling and painful, but they are simply feelings. They are all part of our natural repertoire and can be very useful in helping you grow. I declare all this in the face of the tyranny of positivism that has sprung up in the New Age, where there are rules that tell you which emotions are "appropriate," just as you were told when you were a kid. Upset, anger, and fear have been labeled inappropriate. Dealing with emotion in this way tends to treat everyone but "those in the know" like children who need to be told what is right and wrong, regardless of the fact that emotions flow naturally. In a perfect world you would experience your emotions, express them, and release them. Clearly we live in a less-than-perfect world.

What do you think happens to emotion not expressed? It has to go somewhere, because it's energy. If you don't express it, then you suppress it. It isn't gone, it has just gone unhonored. It has gone underground, where it gathers more energy to explode or implode at a later date. Emotion happens in the body, and so every emotion that goes unexpressed is imprinted there. Your emotional history can be read within your bodies. When you have held grief and sadness for a very long time it actually becomes burdensome, as if you were carrying the weight of the world on your shoulders. Sometimes when you cannot keep your rage down anymore, you are literally unable to keep it down, to stomach it. The rage builds up as bile and acid and finds a physical way out of your body. A lack of loving feelings can often be seen in a pinched face and stiff movements. Often when you have body work done there is a tremendous emotional release. When you do a body detox, your emotions will detox as well.

Terry Lopez was a man whom I worked with as his lover was dying. He had grown up the oldest of several in a very proper Hispanic family. He had always done what he had been expected to do, with the exception of settling down with a woman and having a family. But he and his lover, Ron, had approximated that scenario as closely as possible, so he was still a proper man. He always had a pleasant smile on his face and never seemed to be ruffled. Everything was always all right.

As Ron became ill, Terry became the proper caregiver. He was always attentive, pleasant, and in good spirits. He never expressed any needs of his own nor any feelings about Ron's deteriorating condition or the life that he himself led, which was now totally consumed with the care, feeding, and illness of his closest companion. Terry and I were with Ron when he died. Ron struggled with death. It was a painful experience. As Ron drew his last breaths, I saw Terry's propriety begin to slip away. He just cracked like an egg and all of the feelings he had been holding in came spilling out. They overwhelmed him. He managed to pull himself back together so that he could do a proper job of making the arrangements for the memorial and all of the things that need to be done when a loved one dies. But as soon as all that was over, his emotions began to boil over again. He became reclusive for a while, thinking that he was losing his mind. And in a sense he was. His mind had been keeping his feelings in check for so long that he equated being out of touch with being sane. He had about forty years' worth of bottled-up feelings to release. Once he knew that all he was experiencing was feeling, real live feeling, he got into it. His feelings came flowing forth, they took on the feel of champagne joyously bubbling up, totally uncontrolled, from its containment.

Emotions are physical, not mental—you feel them in your body, and then you think about them, dramatize them, and can focus on them with your mind. But the mind cannot tell you what you feel, since feelings are not a function of the mind. The way you know you are having a particular emotion is that your body has certain sensations that you associate with those feelings. Each person experiences them differently. When I am afraid I get a tingly sensation all over. I feel as though my pores were wide open. The hairs on the back of my neck feel as if they were standing up and I get a chill as my stomach contracts.

Take some time to see how you physically experience various emotions. It will be a useful tool. I will guide you to explore some of your emotions separately, but it is important to keep in mind that they are all part of your natural response to the world and people around you.

It is also important to remember that your feelings may not be related to reality. You may be terrified to ask for something because you have come to fear rejection based on childhood and other adult experiences when in fact, in the present moment, there is no reason to anticipate and fear rejection. What you are feeling is an old fear that rises in response to having to ask for something. Imagine that you are feeling fine as you drive through the country. As you pass a field of flowers you become incredibly sad. As tears well up you wonder why.

Perhaps it is a distant memory of a sad experience triggered by a visual image. What if you are standing in line waiting to get into a film after a brutal day on the job and someone cuts in ahead of you? You explode all out of proportion. Perhaps it is the last straw of a hard day and has little to do with losing your place in line.

At the end of each day, I think it is important to take stock, to give yourself a little time to review the events of the day and see how you responded to them. You will see when your feelings were related to reality, when you overreacted or suppressed yourself. When you suppress an emotion you suppress yourself. When you judge an emotion you judge yourself. You cannot live fully if you live in fear of your feelings. It simply won't work. You can't spend your life managing your feelings. When you cut off the expression of one or more of your emotions for whatever reason, you limit your self-expression. Denial of your emotions, like denial of anything else, gives your emotions more power than they would have if you looked at them, expressed them, and let them go.

You can spend a lifetime suppressing an emotion. Likewise, you can spend a lifetime dramatizing it. What do I mean by dramatizing? Demonstrating it, focusing on it, and calling it back up whenever it appears to be winding down. Revving it up for another go-round. Making sure everyone knows you're having the emotion. That way you can get into the drama, and do not really feel the feelings. It is an external way of avoidance, but the result is the same as suppression. If you allow your feelings to flow in their natural manner and express them, they will come and go. You can have an argument with someone, express your anger, and then moments later be laughing wildly at something wonderful. This is the richness of emotional Mastery.

Fear

Who said there is nothing to fear but fear itself? I'm afraid of everything! It sort of used to get confused with excitement until I got AIDS. Now I can tell the difference. I don't find AIDS particularly exciting!

Jimmie Schaeffer, *Los Angeles, 1986*

FEAR CAN BECOME THE GUIDING PRINCIPAL OF YOUR LIFE, OR IT CAN BE JUST A FEELING. If you live guided by your fear, it can keep you from doing things, and it can make pure hell of the things you do. If you believe your fear, you give it power over you.

There are two kinds of fear. The first is the visceral kind related to reality, such as the heart-pounding and adrenaline rush you undergo when a bear is coming at you at top speed with a hungry look on its face—or the experience of a child sitting there, knot in stomach, waiting to be punished.

The other kind of fear is the perceived fear, fear provoked by a thought or a previous experience. You anticipate that you will be hurt in some way that you have been hurt before. In other words, when you were a child you loved your parents very much but they abused you. It was very painful. Now, as an adult, when you find yourself falling in love you will, out of your childhood fear of being abused, anticipate pain, and so you will stop yourself from loving. Your fear follows a childhood rule that says this is the way it will always be.

Much fear is just anticipation, anxiety. You can't control things, so you fear the worst possible scenario. You focus on the fear and make it feel real. When it feels real enough, it can dictate your responses and behavior.

Say the first time you ever spoke in public you were speaking about a controversial topic. You incurred the wrath of many audience members. You panicked and were so taken aback that during a question-

and-answer session all you could do was defend yourself. Now you have been invited to speak about something that is particularly important to you, but you are sure that you are going to be attacked again and that your viewpoint will be unpopular. You begin to panic every time you think about making the speech. The fear follows you around day after day. No matter how much you tell yourself that that was then and this is now, the fear hangs on. The fear becomes so real that you actually believe that you will be unable to deliver the speech, and cancel the engagement.

Again and again, you will find yourself falling into behavior patterns generated by your fear. You will be stuck in them until you have some physiological experience that it doesn't have to stay that way. Fear is a friend to addiction, for you will let the fear dictate your action until you confront it. The Impostor needs you to believe your fear. The only way to break out of this pattern is to look your fear in the face.

A colleague of mine, psychotherapist Scott Eaton, refers to fear as a hoop of fire. You can stand there paralyzed, entertaining your fear of the fire, thinking about it, wondering about it, and obsessing about it, engaging it. Or you can see the fire and decide it is too dangerous and turn away, letting the fear keep you from going through. The most expanding alternative is to feel your fear and be willing to risk going through the hoop, knowing that once you are through it you will no longer have to be afraid of the fire, or as Susan Jeffries tells us in her book, *Feel the Fear and DO IT Anyway*.

I am afraid of many things. I am often afraid of people but I just acknowledge it and leave my shyness behind in favor of being in the world. I am afraid that I am unworthy of the work I do, but I keep doing it and hope for grace. I am afraid to love because I fear that my heart will be broken. I fear the deaths of my friends and the tremendous loss that those deaths will bring. But fear should not keep us from loving or from living.

This is where we all stand, facing a hoop of fire. We feel the fear of leaving behind the survival that has brought us this far. We feel the fear of losing the Impostor identity that we have come to call by our very own name. We can feel the fear of the unknown. Only by leaping through that hoop of fire can we fully live.

Here is an exercise that will help you to acknowledge, confront, and release your fear. Give yourself plenty of time for this one, and enough privacy to be as noisy as you'd like.

Take a few minutes to energize and center yourself . . .
When you feel relaxed and ready, let your breath deepen.
Take a deep breath right into the places in your body
    where you feel fear.
Let out a sound.
Let the fear fill your body.
See how it affects you.
Just sit with the fear . . .
Take your time and let the feeling flow . . .
What are you afraid of?
What frightens you?
Just let answers emerge . . .
What are you most afraid of right now?
How does this make you feel about yourself?
Take your time . . .

Does it feel familiar?
When you were little, were you scared?
Let yourself feel like a frightened child . . .
How did it feel in your little body?
Let out a sound.
Let yourself feel very small and afraid.
What were you afraid of?
How did you deal with the fear?
Let out a sound.
Who were you afraid of?
What might you need to say to them?
Say it now so you can put these old fears behind you.
Let the little frightened child speak.

Say it all.
Take your time.
Let yourself reexperience your childhood feelings.

Do you sometimes still feel the same as a grown-up?
Let your body feel the fear.
What are you most afraid of?
What do you fear?
Look those fears in the face . . .
Face the fear.
Let the feelings and sound flow.
What else do you fear?
What else?
Take plenty of time . . .
Who do you fear?
What can they do to you?

Let the feelings of fear run through your body
  and imagine doing the thing you fear.
Let your body feel it.
What do you think will happen?
What will they do?
Take enough time to feel the impact.

What happens when you do the thing you fear?
What happens to the fear?
Once the thing you fear is faced, you can release the fear.
Let it go.
Breathe and let it go.
What happens may be beyond our control.
Living in fear is a choice.
You can face your fear and be fully alive.

As you release the fear allow the vibration of life to fill your body.
As you release the fear begin to feel your own power.
As you release the fear feel the freedom.
Feel the energy.
When you are ready, begin to bring your attention back to your
surroundings and open your eyes.

This is a good exercise to use when there is something in your life that you are afraid to embrace. When you seem stuck, look for a hidden fear. It becomes habit for many of us to look for the safe road, the comfortable, often-trod path.

Anger

The anger I feel keeps pouring from this bottomless pit.
I rage against the injustice in the world. I am enraged that
my brothers are loathed and allowed to die. I am furious
that we keep electing unfeeling fools and homophobes. I
am grateful that I can rage in a public forum.

Paul Monette, *Los Angeles, 1990*

YOUR PARENTS ALWAYS TOLD YOU NOT TO BE ANGRY. Your schoolteachers always told you anger was inappropriate. Whenever you displayed your youthful anger, you got into trouble. Anger is one of the most maligned—and necessary—feelings we have. You may go to great lengths to avoid confrontation because you don't want to deal with other people's anger or your own. You hold back your own anger because other people are uncomfortable with it, and so are you.

From toddlerhood you've been told that anger is a negative emotion. Your father might have punished you for displaying your anger. You were told that nice little girls and boys don't get angry. And so you suppressed your anger. You were told that God wouldn't like it if you got angry (though I think God acted out of anger once or twice, according to the Bible), and so you judge your rage.

If you come from a violent or abusive home, you might equate violence and abuse with anger. In fact, violence and abuse are not an expression of anger, but anger *unexpressed* that builds up and explodes. When someone takes a gun and goes into a McDonald's and lets loose with a barrage of gunfire, that is not an expression of anger. When a parent brutalizes a child, that is not an expression of anger. When a nation rises up in violent revolt, that is not an expression of anger. All of these explosions are the result of the consistent *lack* of freedom to express *healthy* anger.

If, when you grew up, your parents yelled and screamed, the

sound of raised voices can throw you back to those childhood moments. And so, as an adult, you will avoid confrontation at all costs. If your parents argued behind closed doors, you may think that anger is inappropriate, private, shameful. All of this affects your relationship to your own anger and rage. As an adult you will act out your anger or hide it away by denying its existence.

It is tough to be clear and current with your anger. In the process of living life within the confines of the malfunctioning systems that have come to define you, you have built up so much rage over the years that it's hard to tell just what it is that you are angry about. It is hard to tell if the anger you feel is related to the present or a reflection of your personal history. Often your angry reaction to things is way out of proportion to the thing itself. This usually happens because much of the charge is from residual anger from similar events in the past. If you had expressed your rage in the past, it wouldn't explode in the present. In other words, when a car cuts you off on the highway and you lose it, screaming obscenities and pounding on your horn, the explosion is not really the fault of an irresponsible stranger in another car. You may also be raging at your lover, your feelings of powerlessness at work, or a childhood anger that has not been expressed. Some button has been pushed, and you blow the lid you had been trying to keep on your rage.

When people walk around in a constant state of rage and explode at the slightest provocation, it isn't the provocation that the rage is about. It has to be more than that. It's about anger that has gone unstated, unattended. It is about unexpressed history. When you are filled with rage it is just that: you are filled. You can't hold any more. If every time you stuffed your rage you stuffed a wad of garbage in a garbage bag, the bag would fill up; when it couldn't hold any more, the seams would split and the garbage would pour out. That is just what happens with your anger—or any emotion—that you stuff inside yourself. It will have to explode somewhere—most likely all over some unsuspecting grocery clerk who gives you the wrong change, or those closest to you. After all, isn't that what friends are for?

And if you don't explode, you'll implode. You may take the anger in and find that it expresses itself as illness. Look at all of the immune-related illnesses that are showing up lately. To be sure, many may be environmentally caused, or they may involve viruses, but what psychological trend might they hint at? The immune system's function is to protect you. Its breakdown is a signal to another kind of breakdown. If you are filled with unexpressed inner anger, you may not think you are worthy of protection or immunity.

Old anger and the residual resentment that it produces are often seen as factors in cancer. We've already discussed the idea of the "cancer personality." The role of suppressed rage as a corollary in other health issues has become accepted.

Anger is a tricky business. Just as you may explode or implode over the buildup of issues from the past, you may act out over things that go unexpressed daily. Say you have this huge fight with your lover about keeping the house clean. It gets really explosive and you get really righteous. Then it gets settled in some fashion. Let's say you win the argument and your lover agrees that you're right, and promises to keep things spotless. If you were really arguing about the house being dirty, then you will both feel great; if, however, what you really wanted to say was that you don't like the way you are being treated and that you feel hurt, that you feel unloved, unseen, and this is how your father treated your mother, then you are stuck with your anger. Telling the truth will set the anger free: otherwise you are left with it to boil up again.

There are lots of other ways to produce suppressed rage. Having too high a set of expectations can provide you with a sure source of anger and frustration. This goes for expecting too much of others and of yourself. Often in the growing-up process, expectations are placed upon you. You may have spent your childhood rebelling against those expectations and failing or refusing to comply, or you may have grown up always trying to be good enough. Either way, you have a tendency to adopt those expectations and behaviors in adulthood.

June, a client of mine, was deeply depressed. She had been offered a very powerful job in the film industry and was expected to do wonders for her company. Though her employer's expectations were high, they were nothing compared to her own. She worked furiously and tirelessly, always demanding much more of herself and her staff than anyone could actually be expected to deliver. She began to grow enraged at herself for not being superhuman and for not producing superhuman results from her staff. This exacerbated the demands she placed on herself and her staff. She would rage and have tantrums.

Eventually things came to a boil and all of her rage had to be addressed.

June had to bring her life to a crisis in order to give herself the time or permission to slow down long enough to look at the real source of her rage. She was never going to be able to live up to the expectations that had been placed on her in childhood.

Only when you can identify the source of your anger can you begin to release it effectively. You can separate the old stuff from the current, the unsaid from the truth, and the fiction from reality. You can begin to find useful channels for the rage that would otherwise cripple you. Your anger can guide you to the things in your life that need to be corrected or changed. If you look at the source of the anger, then choices emerge.

If your anger is really old, you may need to do some very personal therapy or group work to release it. If your anger is about current situations, then it is time to exercise your options about changing the circumstances or changing the way you respond to the circumstances.

A powerful way to use your rage is to turn to the larger picture. You can begin to use your anger to move the political structure so that it reflects the good of humankind rather than its greed and corruption and prejudice. Anger and dissatisfaction can create change and can create freedom. If you were a battered wife you may want to take the rage that you experienced at being victimized and go into the world to help others with a similar situation. If your child was killed by a drunk driver you may put your angry energy into working to tighten up the legal penalties for drinking and driving.

I created the AIDS Mastery Workshop out of my rage at the psychosocial system that awaited those diagnosed with HIV infection and others affected by the crisis. I became an AIDS activist in order to have some influence on the political system.

Paul Monette, author of *Borrowed Time, Afterlife, Halfway Home,* the memoir *Becoming a Man,* which won the 1992 National Book Award, and much extraordinary poetry, has in his soul the same quality of rage that is present in his writing. His rage runs through the words of his characters to the hearts of the readers.

I met Paul shortly after the publication of *Borrowed Time.* We were at a Los Angeles meeting of ACT UP (AIDS Coalition to Unleash Power). The two of us were part of a group of activists who had agreed to support those planning an act of civil disobedience at the Food and Drug Administration building in Maryland. We were to support Steve Kolzak, former first vice president of casting for Embassy/Columbia Television, and the person in the world whose rage at injustice most closely mirrored my own. He was going to get arrested at the FDA. Paul was Steve's new boyfriend. It was delightful to discover that Paul was a fellow traveler.

At the FDA some weeks later, I witnessed what rage can do when it's harnessed and used creatively. Our collective anger was directed at a place where change could be made. For those of us who could no longer bear the injustice of governmental processes that kept necessary drugs from the dying, this was anger with purpose. For us as individuals, this form of activism provides catharsis and empowerment. Because of such activism the FDA has made many changes in its policy and the drug-approval process has opened up. Steve got arrested that day in heroic fashion and Paul fell in love with him. Less than two years later, Paul and I raged together over the death of Steve Kolzak.

There is, however, a great difference between acting up and acting out. If an issue with authority motivates your expression of rage, neither the cause nor your psychological well-being will be served by demonstrating. If your problem is with authority, which most likely reflects your relationship to parents or teachers or others with power over you, then your issue needs to be resolved in a therapeutic setting, not in the streets. If you are acting out your anger in personal relationships, those relationships are the appropriate place to resolve those issues, not the political process. But if you are angry at the system, it will serve both your anger and the opening up of the system to challenge the structure that has damaged you and many others.

Though your anger can be a powerful guide, it also needs to be expressed with responsibility. If you deliver the full charge of your pent-up rage with glass-breaking ferocity, you cannot expect other people to respond in a useful way. They'll probably have to defend themselves. If you are angry at someone and want to be heard, it's a good idea to find some outlet for the charge. Activism for a cause that you believe in is one way. There is also a wonderful moment in the film version of *Cabaret* when Liza Minnelli takes Michael York under a railroad bridge; as the train passes overhead, they scream and scream until the train goes by. What a release!

There are lots of ways to get to the root of old angers so that you can live in the present, filled with the energy that used to go into suppressing or dramatizing your anger. What follows is a visualization that looks at your anger and distinguishes the past from the present.

Get comfortable.

You may want to have some pillows that you can pound on nearby in case the urge arises.

Breathe through your body.

Allow yourself to feel whatever is going on in your body right now.

Let out a sound.

Let your breathing deepen as you ground yourself and let the energies from the earth and universe flow through your body.

Keep breathing deeply.

Let's explore your anger.

Your rage and anger.

Breathe into the places in your body where you feel anger . . .

Where do you experience anger?

How does it affect your body?

Feel it in your body . . .

Where do you feel it?

Just breathe into those places and let up any images that go with the feeling.

See what images come up . . .

What are you angry about?

Who are you angry with?

Take your time . . .

Did someone hurt you?

Did someone tell you that you weren't good enough?

Not enough?

Who said that?

Give yourself plenty of time to discover what it is that enrages
   you . . .
Let the feelings and the images flow . . .
Take your time and breathe deeply . . .
Let yourself discover all that you need to know . . .
Let your body experience the feelings . . .

When you are ready, allow yourself to go back in time.
Did you feel angry as a child?
Did you feel hurt?
Let out a sound.
Now see yourself as an angry little child.
Let yourself be that angry little child.
Let your body fill with the feelings.
Reexperience that time.
What was it like?
What did you do with the feelings?
Who were you angry at?
Are you still angry at them?
Let it out . . .
What do you need to say to them so that you can separate this
   anger from your adult anger?
Let out a sound.
Just keep letting it go . . .
Let it out of your body.
Just keep releasing it from your body.
Get it out of your body where it can't hurt you.
If you are resisting, just breathe through the resistance.
Did someone abuse you?
Did it make you angry?
Did you have to be a grown-up before it was time to be one?
How did that feel?
Are you angry?

Say so!
It's safe to say so.
Let out a sound.
Let your whole body experience the anger.
What does this angry child need to say?
Let the child speak.
Do these feelings feel familiar?
Stay with these childhood feelings until you experience a release.
Have they changed in adulthood?
Let yourself come back into present time.
Does it ever feel like childhood now?
How does it affect your body?
Really feel it.
How do you feel?
Who are you angry at in the present?
Let out a sound.
Do you need to tell them anything?
Tell them now.
Just keep letting it go.
Let it go!
What is it?
What's the anger?
Let it go.
Does someone abuse you?
Who treats you abusively?
Rejects you?
Abandons you?
Hurts you?
Humiliates you?
Does it make you sad and angry?
Feel the anger and let it flow through you . . .
Tell them now.
Don't hold on to this.

Say it all.

Who are you angry with?

Let the anger out where it won't hurt you.

Keep letting out sound.

You deserve to let go of this stuff.

It keeps your life stuck.

Let your body be overwhelmed with your anger.

What is it that you can do with this anger?

Whom do you need to speak to?

How can you direct your anger so that it no longer impairs your well-being?

Let the answers come.

Ask your anger what it has to tell you.

Ask it to guide you . . .

What do you need to know?

Let yourself listen to your wise anger . . .

Let the anger begin to calm.

Let the anger slowly guide you beyond itself . . .

Let your breath slow down and notice if there is a sense of peace that comes with the release.

Ask your anger to keep telling you what you need to know about it and begin to let your breathing become normal.

Imagine that you are wrapped in a peaceful, caressing mist and that it will soothe you as the anger fades.

Let the mist caress away the anger.

Let it absorb the anger.

Allow your breath to bring peace into your body where there was anger.

Let the peace caress you and bring understanding.

Let the information that the anger has brought you be absorbed . . .

Sit with the information and let it be absorbed on a visceral level.
Be still and peaceful.
When you are ready, take your journal and list the things
from the past that have crept into this visualization.
Then list the things in the present that you are angry about
and what can be done about them right now, in the present.

It is well and good to discover the source of your anger but it is far better to take it a step farther. Some of the things that anger us require action. The action may be refusing to allow someone to treat you abusively, writing a letter to the president, or having a conversation with your mother. Remember the Goethe quote? "Whatever you can do or dream you can do, begin it. Boldness has genius, power and magic in it. Begin it now."

There are also actions that can be taken to deal with more generalized feelings of anger. There are primal therapies, Gestalt exercises where you pound pillows, rebirthing practices, and holotropic breathwork that allow you to release pent-up emotion. Some people run or dance or do aerobics. Now, I don't mean to substitute exercise for expressing anger; I mean to consciously use the activities to express what you are feeling. It is possible to have a good relationship with your anger, allowing it to serve you, rather than the other way around.

Sadness

Grief is my constant companion. There's hardly time to deal with the grief of one friend dying, before the news comes of someone else. I am constantly in a state of sadness. It's just there under everything else. I'm sadder now than when I was a kid.

Jaak Hamilton, *Los Angeles, 1987*

MOST OF US POSSESS A DEEP WELL OF SADNESS WE TRY TO IGNORE. The source of this sadness is our separation from our Genuine Selves and our basic core belief in our own unworthiness. We go to great lengths to avoid these feelings, yet they keep rising to the surface.

If you allow yourself to feel your sadness, you will move closer to being healed. You must experience it if you are going to get back to your Genuine Self. This doesn't mean that once you've experienced the sadness you will not feel sad again; there are many things that sadden us daily or pull at our heartstrings. Sadness, like anger, can be a call to action. If the state of the world saddens you, you may be moved to do something about the quality of life on earth. If you are sad enough about the quality of your own life, you may also be moved to action. When you tire of suppressing your sadness or dramatizing it, you will move to shift your experience and the way you hold life. The feelings of sadness can be a guide to what needs to be done in the present and what needs to be released from the past.

Sadness takes many forms and has many names. One of the elements of sadness is disappointment. We all have many expectations and grow up with disappointments. Dad says he'll play with you on Sunday, you'll go to the zoo. Sunday rolls around and Dad has been on a Saturday-night bender. No zoo! You are deeply disappointed and sad. (This is not to say that you are not also angry, and you may begin to create a core belief system based on lack of trust or expectations of disappointment.)

You may also be saddened by how your life has turned out so far. Perhaps you thought that you would have a loving companion but have not yet found someone to share your life. Perhaps you thought that the career you have been pursuing and all of your success would bring you happiness, and instead all it has brought you is success. Things may not be the way you wanted them to be. Perhaps you loved someone and that person died.

Grief is another source of sadness. You grieve almost from birth. You grieve over the loss of the womb, the safety and intimacy there. You grieve over the passing of time and each promise unfulfilled. You grieve for the way you thought life would be and for your failed expectations. You do not usually know you grieve, and so you do not take time to mourn. In order to be current with your grief, I believe it is important to honor these passages, to consciously release them. Each time you let go of a belief system, it is as if it died. Each time you make a transition in your life, it is as if the old had died to make room for the new.

I realized this when I found a photo of my daughter Tracy at two years old. She was adorable, with an enormous smile, wild eyes, and almost no hair. My memories of that time were joyous, and yet I began to feel an incredible grief rising up as I looked at the picture. I couldn't understand it at first and then I realized that I was grieving because that two-year-old is gone. I have a wonderful adult Tracy who brings me great joy, but the two-year-old is in effect dead. I can no longer hold her on my lap. It is too late to be the mother I wanted to be. It is too late to make up for the disappointments that she had to live through. I felt this grief deeply but learned a great deal about passages.

I remember going to my younger daughter Julie's graduation from the Art Institute of Chicago. It was a wonderful day and I was very proud of this wildly talented young woman. Yet under all of the joy, I felt a sadness. Later I realized that I had always wanted to finish art school and live the life of an artist when I was her age. Instead I had opted for marriage. I had never grieved for the loss of my youthful dreams.

It is a good idea to give yourself some time to see what it is that you are grieving over—whether it is the loss of a lover, old disappointments, or even the loss of your false self and your survival tools. (As you have already seen, letting go of the Impostor and your identification with survival is a loss.) Why not give yourself an opportunity to write about each thing that you are letting go of? Each has served you well, ought to be honored and released. Get out your journal. Make a list of all the things that you have lost, large or small, positive or negative. Look over your list and see what you might need to say about these things, people, relationships, and passages. Writing is a powerful tool for release. You can write many things, including letters of farewell and grief.

Loss is a separation, and to the degree that you are attached to the thing or person that you lose, you will feel the impact of that loss and separation. If you identify part of your own sense of self with the person or thing that is gone, you will suffer loss of self along with the actual loss. When this happens you can grieve on two levels —for the event itself and for yourself.

Paul Monette has AIDS now and falls periodically into illness. The thought of losing him fills me with anticipatory sadness. My sadness exists on two levels. The first is that the world can little afford the loss of such brilliance. The other level is personal. Aside from the fact that I love him, I feel as if there exists a person who actually knows what it is like to live in my skin; if he were to die I would lose a witness to my experience of life.

When you anticipate loss you may be taken out of the present. Being caught in the anticipation of loss keeps you from the pleasure of the moment and renders the loss operative before it ever happens. You can learn to honor these feelings without falling prey to them.

Being around AIDS has left many of us with little time to grieve. Even as you bury a friend, you plan to visit another in the hospital, only to go home and get a message of another impending disaster on your phone machine. A friend of mine calls it grief on the run. Many of us have lost the friends and loved ones that made up our daily lives; not only do we miss them, but our lives are not the same without them. Knowing that we can call upon a loved one's spirit is comforting, but we still can't call that person to dish on the phone or go to a movie.

A young girl I met in a New York workshop has AIDS. She had her first child when she was fourteen and became an addict that same year.

She has had two children since. The littlest one has already died of complications of AIDS, and her middle child is infected. She lives in a constant state of grief. She grieves for the child that she has lost, the one she may lose soon, and the one she may leave behind. Of course, all of the grieving is compounded by her sadness at having carried this virus to her children. She feels forever deeply connected to her dead child on a spiritual level, but she cannot hold the sweet baby in her arms and watch her grow up. Her expectations as well as her heart are shattered. Left unacknowledged, all that grief could undermine her health, well-being, and the time she has to be with her children.

Grief is a very full and rich and ultimately very nurturing emotion. The part of grief that causes pain can be released so that what we feel when we recall a loved one is the love and sweetness rather than our own pain and guilt. When people die we do not have to allow part of ourselves to die with them; we can remain whole and hold their memories dear to our hearts.

There is an even more basic kind of sadness you can experience, a sadness about who you are, or rather who you think you are. The sadness can so permeate your being that it underlies whatever else you feel. It becomes your core sense of yourself. You become a "sad person." There can be such deep sadness for your sense of worthlessness and shame that you virtually live in a state of mourning for your Genuine Self.

This visualization will help you to discover the source of your own sadness, honor the passages in your life, experience the grief that you have stored up, and release it as part of the healing process.

Find a comfortable place to nest.

Put on some music.

Grab a box of tissues.

Begin to let your breath deepen.

Be with the rhythm of your breath, the vibration from the center of the earth and the infinite universe.

Begin to direct your breath to the places in your body where you feel sadness.

Where do you feel it?

Breathe into those places where you feel the sadness . . .
Let your body be overwhelmed with sadness . . .
Some of it is new.
Some is very old.

Is some of the sadness disappointment?
Who disappointed you, failed you?
Let out a sound.
Take your time and allow images to appear.
Be there with your feelings and your images . . .
Who have you disappointed?
Just let the feelings come up.
Let out a sound.
Let the feelings in.
Just let yourself feel.
What did you expect?
What had you hoped for?
Has it been so disappointing?
Just let the sadness come up.
Let out a sound.

And what about loneliness?
When do you feel lonely?
Take your time.
Is this how it was when you were little?
Were you left alone physically or just emotionally?
Who abandoned you?
Who made you sad?
What do you need to say to them?
Say it now.
Let yourself be that sad little child . . .
Let yourself feel like that sad child . . .

Let the child speak . . .
Take all the time you need.
What made you sad?
Who made you sad?
Stay with it until you are ready to come back into the present . . .

When is it like this in the present?
Let yourself feel the sadness.
The loss.
What have you lost?
Let the images and the feelings flow . . .
Have you lost your dreams?
Is this the way you thought your life would be?
Just let those feelings of grief come up.
What are you grieving for?
Who are you grieving for?
Who have you lost?
Let them appear . . .
One by one, begin to see those for whom you grieve.
You may grieve for those who have died or for relationships
  lost . . .
Spend time with them . . .
Speak to them . . .
What do you want to say to them?
Give yourself time to speak to them, to be with them.
Just be there with your loss.
Look into their faces.
Take time to see them, breathing deeply . . .
What do you want to tell them?
Just be with them.
Keep letting out sound.
And those for whom you've had no time to grieve.
And those whose loss you wouldn't let yourself feel?

Who do you fear losing?
What do you want to say to them?
Let out a sound.
Just tell them so it won't be too late for them to hear it.
Who else do you fear losing?
Really let yourself feel . . .

Begin to breathe deeply into your feelings
        and allow yourself to grieve for yourself.
The passing of time.
The passages in your life . . .
Each time you make a transition or grow, you leave part of your
    life behind.
Allow yourself to mourn the loss . . .
In this grief lies the ability to move on to the richness of the
    present and the promise of the future.

Begin to allow an image of yourself to appear . . .
Just be there with yourself.
Look into your eyes.
Know that as your Genuine Self emerges the Impostor must leave.
See if you need to grieve for this loss, this passage.
The Impostor has served you well but it is time to let it go.
As you do you can embrace life fully.
Let your feelings flow.
Let that light surround and comfort you and bring you back into
    the present.

Joy

I always thought that I was happy. With enough booze and dope I could always have a good time. Of course, now that I am clean and sober, it has occurred to me that if I had to get drunk to enjoy myself, it probably wasn't such a good time after all. I really feel joy in my life now.

Danny Adams, *Los Angeles, 1988*

People can't understand how I could always be in such rage and grief and still be having such a joyous life.

Paul Monette, *Los Angeles, 1990*

JOY IS ONE OF THE EMOTIONS THAT WE COME BY NATURALLY. We are born with it. When a baby is satisfied it is full of joy. Joy, contentment, and happiness are its natural state. If baby isn't wet, hungry, afraid, or hurt in some way, it feels just fine. Yet pure joy gets farther and farther from our grasp as we move farther from our true selves. Joy erupts from feelings of well-being and satisfaction from within—and those feelings can be far too rare among adults.

If your childhood is difficult, it is difficult for you to experience a lot of unbridled joy as you grow up. It then follows that this is so in your adulthood. Not that you don't have moments of ecstasy and rapture, but I think that you are meant to have that experience a good amount of the time rather than in little bursts because something outside yourself has stimulated it.

You come to rely on others, on outside stimuli, or on substances for joy and pleasure. I did a lot of that. At some point it occurred to me, as it did to Danny, whom I quoted, that if I were really having a good time, if I were really happy, it wouldn't take cocaine, booze, and a romance to make me feel happy.

If you sensed that you were the same kind of miracle of nature and were in touch with the beauty of your own spirit, the joy you get from looking at brilliant rainbows and beautiful scenery could actually be felt when you looked in the mirror. Joy is an excitement at being alive. Joy is an excitement at being yourself. You are so unaccustomed to feeling it without a reason that you have come to accept numbness or lack of pain as a substitute, as normal. You assume a sort of neutral state that passes as acceptable. You need something to make your heart full rather than allowing your heart simply to be full because you deserve to feel that way. You think of joy as a response to "something" rather than as a response to just being in touch with your spiritual source, which expresses itself from within.

Joy may have become a stranger to you. True happiness has come to mean lack of stress rather than actual rapture. You don't even trust people who express too much joy. It is somehow disconcerting to ask people how they are and have them say, "Wonderful!" You can accept "all right," and are used to "not so good," but "wonderful!" What is that? People who declare that must be lying or on drugs.

Now, "on drugs" is how many of you, like me, used to feel good. You would think that you felt good about yourself and so you would think you were having a real good time. You had the thought that you were experiencing joy. The problem was that the joy, and the behavior that you thought brought you joy, came when you were suppressing your sadness and feelings of inadequacy with a substance. A substance or activity is not joy, it is a substitute for joy.

Doing the right thing won't bring happiness if you are doing it to be a good boy or girl. Winning at something isn't a happiness substitute. It will bring joy to a joyous person. It will bring only temporary relief to others. Service can bring great happiness if you serve in order to give from your fullness. If you serve to fill up it won't work.

In realigning with the self there is joy on the natch. It is quite different and can begin to replace feelings of worthlessness as the gap narrows. This will hold true if you are at work or if you are at play. Contemporary society is not set up for most people to have a good time in the everyday working world. The nature of work, as society has embraced it, has left little room for joy. Far too few of us love our work. Most people wait to play until they leave work. (If in fact they can leave their work behind.) When the serious part of the day is over, you relax, let your hair down, and "become yourself." Well, who do you think went to work? When you finish work you can play. In this scenario, even playing right seems like work. If you love your work and it brings you joy, you don't burn out. If you feel joyous about yourself, work works and a vacation becomes something to do to bring more joy rather than something you need to replace your everyday feelings.

Many of us never really experienced uninhibited play as children. Those of you who did probably thought it had to go when you grew up. A good time is something that is reserved for special occasions or weekends. Now, I don't mean that you all should turn around and behave like children, but I do urge that you tap into the freedom that your "real self" child had, even if the Impostor child never acted it out, and begin to experience joy as a ground of being.

It is unrealistic to expect to feel joy all of the time. That is not possible without denying the painful realities of life and the enraging and saddening experiences that you have. You need to be wherever you are emotionally. The more fully you do that without interrupting your feelings with thought patterns and judgments, the more fully and richly your emotional life will unfold. This is true of your joy, too.

I quoted Paul Monette at the beginning of this section. In the world of AIDS there is much to rage against. It is possible to rage against an inept and uncaring government and get great joy from doing so. Though Paul is enraged, he expresses that rage fully, and though he often feels ill, he often feels great joy. I know that this is true for myself as well. With all of the pain and death and suffering that I am around, I also have amazing, joyous experiences. The people that I work with, though very sick, will call upon a deep humor and a deep spirituality that brings them joy and enriches them and me.

In being with people as they die, it is amazing to observe the struggle end. As their lives slip away, a peaceful spirit enters. With this spirit comes the joy of release and surrender. In life, as in death, I would think that one of the surest roads to joy is surrender. Surrender to whatever the moment presents. Surrender and gratitude can lead the way to joy.

When you suppress your feelings of rage or sadness or unworthiness, you also suppress your joy. There is a logic that leads you to believe that if you could push down your fear or self-loathing, you would be able to feel joy. Not so. Our bodies don't really know how to suppress one thing without automatically reducing the experience of everything else. Remember what we discussed in terms of trying to be in control. The illusion of control can cost you peace and joy. If you are engaged in fighting down your feelings, you have no time for joy. There is joy in acceptance of the truth. When I forget, I can remind myself by reciting the Serenity Prayer.

G*od, grant me the serenity*
to accept the things I cannot change,
the courage to change the things I can,
and the wisdom to know the difference.

Happiness is your birthright, and yet it is very hard to allow yourselves to "be" happy. But why should something that is so natural and feels so good be so difficult to embrace? The bottom-line answer is that your addiction doesn't want you to be happy. It will let you have a tease. It will let you have the false happiness of a substance high. It will let you fall madly in love. It will let you enjoy a breathtaking sunset. The addiction will give you a taste but will bar you from having joy as your life source. It certainly doesn't want you to think you deserve it or get too used to it. It wants circumstances to dictate your happiness and it wants to dictate the circumstances and the amount of joy you are allotted. If you know you deserve joy and in fact experience it as your ground of being, what happens to the Impostor? If you are happy, how will you stay in touch with your ancient self-loathing? The answer is, you won't.

If you can embrace your pain and fear and sadness and see it as just a part of life and growth, you will move closer to joy. If you allow your feelings, whatever they are, to come through you, if you can experience them fully and be grateful for feeling, you are even closer. I often think, "I hate this feeling, but at least I am feeling." I am grateful for feeling. I feel closer to myself and to spirit and to joy when I feel. This would not be possible for me without tapping into a joy from within.

One way to begin to discover that you can be the source of your own joy is to see yourself that way. To do this you will have to sit or stand in front of the mirror again.

Close your eyes for a moment.
Reconnect to the energies from the center of the earth
and the infinite universe or whatever brings you into your
process.
Take your time . . .
Allow yourself to go back to a time during the day
(or whatever day it was) when you felt joy.
When you had a good time.
When you might have laughed and laughed.
Keep your eyes closed and let the memory come up . . .
Breathe into all of the places in your body where you felt the joy.
Reexperience the joy.
Let it come up in your body.
Let it just flow through you.
Let out a sound and just let the feelings come up.

What was it that you felt joy over?
What brought you this feeling?
Now let yourself remember other experiences of joy.
Let the feeling of rapture flow through your body.
When did this happen?
Who was there?
Where were you?
Allow yourself to keep that sensation.

Drift back in time to your childhood.
Let yourself remember a time when you were a child
and had great joy, had a great time!
Let those feelings come up.
Remember having fun, being in joy!
What brought you those feelings of joy?
What made you happy?

Feel the happiness . . .
Let it flow through your little body.
Let yourself feel like a happy child.

Does it feel the same as now?
It is happening in the same body.
You are the common denominator in the experiences.

Keep breathing into the feeling and open your eyes.
Look at yourself in the mirror.
Keep breathing into the feelings.
See the joy on your face.
See it in your body.
Feel it all over.
This is your joy!
It is your experience.
It is your choice.
When you feel a release, breathe that joy through you, sit for a
*   moment.*
Go about your business, bringing the joy into your activity.

It may be that when you look for the joy you will come up with other feelings. Sometimes sadness comes up, or you sense a lack of joy. The joy is there. It may just be so buried under rage or sadness or fear or shame that it will take a while to reconnect with it. Just trust. Once you connect to it, joy can become the underlying emotion of your life.

No matter how far adrift the circumstances of your life may take you, you can experience gratitude and joy as the central force, nurturing your Genuine Self. When this happens, your anger and sadness will not turn to despair, resentment, and bitterness. When this shift happens you will see life as a more powerful expression not of limitations but of possibilities.

Love

My heart wants love, but my head doesn't think it can ever have it.

Franke Piazza, *Los Angeles, 1989*

WHEN YOU SPEAK OF LOVE, YOU REALLY SPEAK OF TWO DIFFERENT TYPES. One kind is conditional love and one is unconditional. Much of the love that you give has strings attached to it. Romantic love is more conditional than almost anything else in life. We will discuss that later on when we take on relationships.

As children, so many of us have to learn the system and strategies of survival that to some extent we lose sight of what love really is. You think that if you are good enough, smart enough, interesting enough, cute enough, or do things right, you will be loved. You may think that love comes as a reward or in some form of abuse. You may think that love is being allowed to be unabused. Childhood sets the stage for our relationship with love, and make no mistake about it, we all do have a relationship with love. You worry about it, plan how to get it, and spend enormous amounts of energy trying to *earn* it. Enormous amounts of energy also go into trying to figure out how to *give* love.

These are exercises in futility, because before you can learn to love and accept love, you must unlearn the behavior patterns that you have developed around love. The process begins by accepting that you are lovable. Only then can you accept love without working for it and give love freely without guarantees.

If you feel unloved as a child and assume the identity of "unlovable," your behavior patterns will drive you to great lengths to prove yourself worthy of love. (Or to prove yourself perpetually unworthy.) Until your strings to the past are cut, you will follow the rules that you set down in childhood. You will withhold love because you are afraid, or you will be willing to give of yourself until there is nothing left to give. You will manipulate, threaten, and sacrifice, or you will pretend.

Have you ever said "I love you" to someone who says "Thank you" in return? If what you meant was, I love *you*, then the answer is satisfying; you know the other person has received your gift of love. But if what you meant was, "Do you love *me*?" then you were probably devastated by a reply of thanks and left with your unasked question, "But what about me?" When you really love someone saying "I love you" is not about you.

It is tricky business to begin to distinguish between love and need. Yes, we all need love, but as with everything else, the love of someone else will not compensate for the love of self. The adulation of millions will not substitute for self-love. Without self-love you will not think you are deserving, and the love shown to you by others will never sink in. Without self-love it is hard to give love away. You can be loving in your behavior and do loving things, but it is impossible to give what you don't have. The love will ultimately be contingent on how you feel about yourself.

That explains some of the issues that surround conditional love, but what is this stuff called unconditional love? It requires being totally present in the moment and free of your patterns of dysfunction and need. There is a lot of talk about it in the spiritual world, where you are given a lot of rules to follow: just send them loving thoughts, just send them light, just love your enemy. How do you do all that?

If you can see who other human beings are, you can recognize the essential souls in them, the Genuine Selves, and love them. This is unconditional love. I love you because you *are*.

Now, let me be very clear about this. You can learn to love unconditionally. This does not mean that you will want to eat a meal with everyone you meet. Love and like are not the same thing. In order to love unconditionally, you do not have to give up your discretionary faculties. You do not have to abandon your right to choose your relationships and the kind of behavior that you allow in your life. Love can be unconditional and you may well have conditions on friendship. You may be unwilling to have friendships with people who can't be intimate and truthful. You may not want to have a friendship with someone who is a practicing substance abuser or who abuses you. This does not imply judgment, it simply allows you to create healthy boundaries. You have the right to fill your life with people who nourish you and bring you joy.

You can love people's souls and choose not to play with their personalities. You can accept unconditionally who they are and not their behavior. You are allowed choices and taste! In other words, you can love people and not love their shoes. What is important to know is that people are not their shoes or their behavior, or their Impostors.

The despots of the world have at their core a Genuine Self that is so far out of touch with their own humanness that they exercise their will cruelly over others. They may cause wars, slaughter other humans, wreak havoc on society—and feel justified in doing so. Psychoanalyst and author Alice Miller has written about how Hitler's childhood molded his adult behavior. It is fascinating reading. She talks about the kind of discipline that was practiced in Germany as fertile ground for the monstrous brutality of the Holocaust. The seeds of extermination were planted generations before an advocate arose from the ashes of abuse to render abuse on others.

Closer to home, look at what happened in Los Angeles, where riots have torn through denial. That city has been victimized by a lack of love. That lack of love allowed conditions for the poor to become outrageous and out of control. That lack of caring in Los Angeles and across the country grew from a period in our history when profit took precedent over human concerns. Discrimination and bigotry are being put forth as the political agenda of the religious right, and the environment is being murdered by self-interest. None of this is about love. The perpetrators do not behave in a loving manner.

Yet within the souls of the Hitlers of the world are beings capable of loving another human, fine music, art, and children. They are capable of loyalty and humor. These capabilities are all that remain of a Genuine Self that is so clouded in amnesia that there is no prayer of it resurfacing. There is such deep self-loathing that only loathing on a grand scale can reflect it.

The more you nurture your Genuine Self, the more in love you are going to be with the world *and* with yourself. Unconditional love is easy as long as you are easy on yourself and see that being in human form has made all of us limited. You are not supposed to be transcendent on earth and so you have taste and limits and boundaries. Because you are human you do not like everyone or everything about everybody. You don't need to in order to love them unconditionally.

Sit quietly and comfortably.
Close your eyes and reconnect to the energies
  from the earth and the infinite universe.
Let the energies vibrate within you.
Allow yourself to feel a warmth surrounding you . . .
A safe, comforting warmth.
Now let yourself wander to a place where you feel safe,
  a place where you feel powerful . . .

Bring into that space people whom you find it hard to love.
They can be public figures for practice,
  but later you will want to bring in those closer to you.
Just be with them.
Look into their eyes and think of the behavior
  that you find unacceptable.
Let your feelings flow freely.
Keep looking into their eyes and see if you can imagine
  the source of their behavior.
What could cause them to act in such a manner?
What could have happened to them to create such behavior?
Ask them.
Let them tell you . . .
Let them tell you what it feels like to be them.
Why they behave the way they do.
See if you can begin to separate their Genuine Selves
  from their behavior.
Keep looking into their eyes and breathe deeply into your own
  compassion.
See if you can send them your compassion
  and find their Genuine Selves worthy.
They are not their behavior or history, any more than you are.
Can you find compassion for both of you?

Can you see that their beings are worthy of love
  though their behavior may be intolerable?
You may need to do this more than once to be able to clear the
  path with a particular person.
It is important to be able to discern the difference between
  who people are and how they act.
It is a blessing to do this for yourself.

Love will set you free, just like the truth.

The more in love you can become with yourself, and the more love that you can accept and believe from outside, the more your Impostor will cease to be who you are. When you finally know that you are deserving of love, your painful history becomes a path to self-knowledge rather than a description of who you are. Your self-love is your last holdout. When you tap into it, you walk surely forward into Mastery.

Mastering Sex, Intimacy, and Relationships

Mastering Sex, Intimacy, and Relationships

I *spent most of my life looking for love in all the wrong places. All I ever wanted was a relationship with someone who would love me enough to never leave me. I was so afraid of being alone that I would be with anyone. I have no idea what a relationship is. I would have sex with someone and confuse that physical bonding with closeness and then plunge right into a relationship.*

Genell Roberts, *San Francisco, 1989*

THE CHALLENGES OF LOVE, SEX, INTIMACY, AND RELATIONSHIPS CROSS ALL RACIAL, ECONOMIC, GENDER, AND CULTURAL BARRIERS. The challenges they present most often occur in the form of patterns. Until you can see these patterns and dissolve them, you are doomed to repeat your history. Until you confront your issues around sex, and sexuality, until you discover why the intimacy you long for is so frightening, until you can see why relationships always seem to be the playground for all your other life issues, your Impostor will use your relationships as a hook to your past.

In this portion of *Life Mastery* we will explore and explode some of your personal myths around sex and sexuality, as well as cultural and religious myths that surround these perfectly natural parts of life. Sex is almost always shrouded in some sort of mystery or mystique that makes it seem anything but natural. We all have complicated relationships with our own sexuality and sexual history. For some of us that history includes incest or abuse, for others a shroud of silence and neglect. It is important to pierce through the anxiety, secrecy, shame, and blame that surround sex so that sex can take its functional place in the natural order of daily life.

Sex often plays an important and confusing role in relationships, particularly the kind of relationships that we refer to as intimate. This is the reason that we explore these three areas of life together. They are interwoven but are created from very different threads. As this section progresses you will be able to untangle the confusion that often makes you think you are in love, when in fact you are in the throes of desire and attraction, or think you are intimate with someone when in fact you withhold your Geniune Self.

Much of the same mythology that surrounds sex also surrounds the idea of relationships. You are told as you grow up that you will find "the one" who will make life all right for you. You have grown up thinking that you are not enough on your own. The burden of expectations placed on what you term intimate relationships almost precludes intimacy. This section will challenge these notions and guide you to creating nurturing, fulfilling, and powerful relationships based in reality rather than Hollywood promises with television dialogue. We will look at how rich, rewarding, and intimate relationships can be.

We will also look into your ability to be intimate with others and, most importantly, with yourself, and how to restore that capacity. If you are to expect to live intimately with others, you must not be afraid to be in intimacy with yourself. Intimacy means living in your own truth and not having to hide those things about yourself that you think might not wash well with another. Once you can do that, you are truly available for intimacy.

This section will begin by exploring sex, because believe it or not, it is the easiest of the challenges that we face around all of these issues. The exercises that follow are designed to give you the tools to know and to be true to yourself, so that you know what it is that you want when you seek intimacy in your newly Masterful life.

Sex

Intimacy was scary. Sex seemed easy!

Genell Roberts, *San Francisco, 1989*

ANYTHING THAT STANDS BETWEEN YOU AND THE NATURAL FLOW OF YOUR SEXUAL ENERGY IS WHAT I WOULD CALL A SEXUAL DISORDER. Sexual energy is part of your self-expression and a means of relating to other people, whether you have sex with them or not. Sexual energy is part of your spiritual energy. You are born with it. It is not some lascivious drive but a part of your makeup as a human being.

In a well-integrated person, sexual energy is one of the many facets of energy that radiate from his or her Genuine Self. Performers who keep you on the edge of your seats and keep you coming back for more have the quality of charisma that comes from an expression of sexual energy that is well integrated with other human energies. In a very real way, the magnetism that you experience in the presence of many true gurus is the experience of all energies, including sexual energy, powerfully flowing through them and empowering you. They may be celibate; that's not the point. They radiate their power. Great teachers can do that. Great performers can do that. Everyone can do that.

This kind of integration is difficult to experience as you grow up because sex is treated separately from the socialization process that you went through as a child. In fact, you were never really socialized around sex. More likely you were tyrannized, moralized to, or kept in the dark.

Earlier we looked at the idea that as a child you were allowed to play with just about anything except your body and those of others. Imagine, if you will, a world where children were actually told the truth about sex. Imagine a world where children were allowed to explore their bodies and to touch and feel themselves in any way that would not harm them physically. Imagine a world in which parents told their children that they knew masturbation felt good, but that it made a lot of people uncomfortable, so it would best be done in private. Imagine a world where children were told as much as they could understand about sex when they asked questions; imagine the information being given as a wonderful gift. What if, when children were ready, they were told that sex had two purposes, one being procreation and the other pleasure, and that certain responsibilities and risks came with the territory?

For a while it was chic for parents to be very permissive with their kids about sex. In the name of being modern, and as a reaction to their own restrictive upbringing, they gave their kids no real guidelines or information. They spent time with parents who were naked and sexual. In many cases, healthy limits were left unset in the name of freedom, and children need healthy limits.

If your introduction to sex was the childhood trauma of incest or abuse, the shroud of fear and confusion is very thick. It becomes extremely difficult to separate the feelings that accompanied the abuse from the act of having sex. It colors every facet of relationships and dictates the quality of your sex life, sometimes subtly and sometimes blatantly, until the shroud can be lifted.

Your adult life, feelings, and sexual behavior would have been very different if you had been offered the guidance of parents who were comfortable with their sexuality and their sexual expression. Your relationship to your sexuality would have been completely different if you had grown up in a society where sex was accorded the place in the natural scheme of things that it deserves. Humans are sensual beings. You are born with the capacity for great tactile pleasure. The sense of satin or a cool breeze against your skin brings great sensual delight. Feelings of sexuality are often aroused by your natural sensuality. It would have been wonderful if, along with your sexuality, sensual pleasure had also been treated as a natural extension of the senses.

Most of you, however, have experienced very dysfunctional relationships to your sensuality and your sexuality that grew from the warped training of a rigid system. The importance of sex becomes blown out of proportion because you are offered so little real information and there are so many misunderstandings and taboos.

Generation after generation, we grow up starved for love, needing approval, and longing for intimacy. Because you are not trained in the skills required to know that these are the things that you want or how to get them, you get confused. Many find refuge in sex. Sex becomes a way to get feelings of love or approval, or to substitute for those feelings. The painful confusion creates chaos in adolescence, chaos that often spills over into adult life.

In your search for approval, sex is a major means of finding what you think you need. If someone wants to have sex with you then you must be attractive, worthy, and desirable. Surely if someone (or many someones) wants you, then you must have value. Sex is no substitute for self-worth, but sometimes it will fool you. You may need to be held, to experience affection. Your Impostor will give you sex instead and you may gratefully accept it. Some people become addicted to it.

It is easy to confuse a need for love with a desire for sex. It is easy to feel intimate when you are physically intimate. So often, when the need for love, caring, and intimacy is great, you will opt for sex. There is intense "feeling" stirred up in sex. It "feels" intimate. You "feel" open and vulnerable and full. It "feels" as if you are very close to the person you are having sex with and so it is easy to think that you are emotionally close. But sex is never a real substitute for love or intimacy.

That isn't to say that you can't have sex, love, and intimacy all at once. You can. You can have great sex with someone that you love and are intimate with, but love, sex, and intimacy are three separate items. One won't replace another.

If you have romantic feelings and are attracted to someone, sex can feel like love. The physical closeness and bonding give a good impression of "being in love." We think if sex is great we are in love.

I watched my friend Genell fall madly in love with the most beautiful man I'd ever seen. She knew she was in love. They spent hours having sex. It all seemed perfect. She would admit that every once in a while he would say something or other that would make her uneasy, but minutes later she would forget all about it and become lost in his physical beauty.

Somewhere about a year down the road this beauty got sick. Too sick for romance and too sick for sex. Suddenly they were faced with hours and days of time together. Time to talk. They had clearly been so swept away with the illusion that sex was love and intimacy that they had heard very little of what the other really felt about life. They had missed the fact that other than their wild attraction to each other there was no reason for them to be together. They had both used sex as a substitute for intimacy.

Sex for the sake of sex can bring you much pleasure if that is what you want. But if what you want is intimacy and love, you are out of luck. It seems that society almost forces the illusion of a relationship on people who want to enjoy each other physically. Everywhere the messages that we receive about sex and romance and intimacy add to the confusion. We are told by the advertising industry that if we turn someone on with our smile, our scented armpits, our car, our pumped-up bodies, or our coffee, they will want to have sex with us and spend the rest of their lives in bliss with us. We are sold everything from soup to art with sexual images. We are bombarded with sexual stimulation, erotic films, and videos. Sex and violence and love are all offered up as the stuff of fantasies and also as a model for real life.

On the other hand, we have been told by the dysfunctional social systems that we grow up within that there is something wrong with sex. We are told that sex is for procreation, not pleasure, and that pleasure seekers and sinners are one and the same. We live in an age when sex can pass along a terminal disease, and still sex education is a taboo and the preaching of abstinence is looked upon as a moral imperative. Sex and morality have been entangled for years. We are told that God wants us to abstain from sex until marriage and then to have sex primarily for the purposes of having children. Children are sacred. Sex is profane.

This morality is even harsher in its judgment of same-sex activities, which are thought to be unnatural by all of those who claim to have an inside track on being good, moral, upstanding, God-fearing people.

Same-sex attraction exists in nature. What nature has created cannot be unnatural. What threatens the ego of humans, however, can be labeled unnatural. Nature works very well. If the only reason sexual attraction existed in nature were for procreation, then I feel sure nature would have limited our sex drives to serve just that purpose.

Look at the animal world. It is a much clearer expression of nature, as it is not clouded with ego and psychological fear. Take your average dog. When a male dog procreates, it does so with a member of the opposite sex. When this dog feels sexual it will hump any old dog that will play, or even any old leg or fire hydrant. This doesn't drive the dog to the shrink crying that he has lusted after another male dog, or worse yet an inanimate object. He is not persecuted by other dogs. The dog is doing what comes naturally. We humans don't allow ourselves that right.

There is a body of information that indicates sexual orientation is probably decided genetically. Heterosexuality, while probably also genetically determined, is culturally prescribed as well. I was programmed to be a heterosexual. Anything else was looked upon as a deviation. The stigma still attached to homosexuality is an appalling reminder of how far we have moved away from the reality of nature.

Historically, homosexuality and bisexuality have been no big deal. Heterosexuality has been used as a political and religious tool to manipulate and create what would be perceived as a manageable society. If we look to ancient cultures before monotheism, sexuality was not an issue to be dealt with in the name of God. Homosexual unions were offered as a celebration of the gods. Sparta, one of the civilizations we hold up as an example of masculinity, was a bisexual society, or rather a society in which sexual orientation was not an issue. Ancient Romans encouraged their gladiators to know one another sexually, as it added excitement to the game. Women also found tenderness and compassion and excitement in one another. With the popularization of monotheism in Western society came the idea of rule by fear, guilt, and damnation. And so, all over the world, since we lost touch with our true natures, men in secret make love to men, and women to women. And as within any dysfunctional family, the human family denies it, makes it wrong, shuts down, feels guilt, pain, and loss of self.

The vehemence with which hatred is leveled at the gay and lesbian community by the fundamentalist fearmongers is astounding. The level of vitriol and violence allowed to be perpetrated against a segment of our population that has done nothing more than dare to express themselves is frightening. The religious right needs a target for their hatred and a ploy for fund-raising. And so they choose gays to replace blacks as the object of their fear and loathing. They use gay rights as an issue to replace their failed Right to Life campaign. Because of society's dysfunction around sex, they are able to persecute an entire group of people in the name of God.

The sexual system is self-perpetuating in its dysfunction; any sex that does not support the system must be outlawed, marginalized, and stigmatized. The finger pointing, gay bashing, and homophobic rhetoric exposes an all-consuming prejudice that comes from childish, uninformed fears and generations of indoctrination. It seems that any group that is not sure of their own worth needs to keep another group down.

While some of us knew our sexual orientation very young and never doubted it, others of us shift and make discoveries later in life. I had grown up in a world where I was simply expected to date boys and eventually marry one and settle down. I did that. I was a heterosexual and that was that. Being anything else simply never entered my mind. So discovering that I was bisexual was a great surprise. It was late in my marriage. I was sitting in a restaurant in London, on vacation with my former husband, when in walked Julie Christie and Warren Beatty. Suddenly, I could barely breathe. I flushed. I was tingling all over and seemed to move outside myself. I lost my appetite, which for me was alarming. Suddenly I realized that I was overwhelmingly turned on— not by him, though he certainly exudes sexual energy, but by *her*.

Only years later, when I began to get enough sense of who I was, did I allow my attractions to have a natural life of their own. I became aware of a greater range of expression. I became aware that there were many more choices available. Expressing our sexual energy comes as naturally as breathing; it is one of our ways to relate to other human beings.

I was lucky. My sexual expression didn't seem to ruffle anyone's feathers or become problematic for me. I had already begun to discover my Genuine Self and to find pride in my expression of that self. I did not have to grow up hearing myself vilified or dealing with the traumas of maturing with no role models to reflect my sexual feelings. I did not have to negotiate my life through the hatred of a narrow-minded system. I did not have to grow up with my Impostor teaching me sexual self-loathing because I was different.

In reality we human beings are comprised of a blend of yin and yang, anima and animus, creative and receptive, male and female energies. It would seem clear that a balance among these energies would bring you close to your spiritual self and your Genuine Self. The perfect melding of these energies would be an androgynous state of balance. It is imperative that in order to grow, you look to your own sexual truth—not so that you change your sexuality, not so that you can be different, but so that you can be comfortable with your sexuality and having sex.

Again I want to offer an exercise. I don't care how free and how liberated we think we are; unless we have faced the dragons that stalk our genuine sexual selves, we are still prey to them. The dragons were put in place long ago. We may have forgotten them, but within us they still breathe fire.

When I was a girl my mother said that "nice girls don't!" And so after my divorce, when I set out to have adventure, explore sex, and compensate for years of monogamy, I became "not nice"! In fact, I became compulsive! I was looking to satisfy my desire for intimacy, self-worth, closeness, and acceptance. I thought I was liberated, but in the back of my head, with each encounter with a man or woman, the shifting morality that I had been raised with undermined not only my pleasure but my self-love. Our early learning is tough to detach from. For those who have been sexually abused it is even harder to detach the memory or feelings from present sexual relationships. The Impostor wants these memories and feelings to stay in place.

Let's look at where voices from the past may be inhibiting your self-love and your relationship to your sexuality and your overall Genuine Self. It is imperative that to do this you return to the innocence of childhood, before the imprint of the system is made. In this way you can rediscover your sensuality and your sexuality. You can grant yourself the joy of experiencing your sexuality as your right and privilege, a joyous expression of your spirituality.

Get yourself very comfortable.
Create a very safe space where you will not be disturbed.
Breathe through your body.
Allow energy to flow through you.
Begin to become aware of your body.
Be aware of any tension that you are holding.
Imagine that your breath is soothing energy . . .
Send your breath to the places that you are feeling tension
  and begin to massage those areas with your breath . . .
Really feel your body.
Let your breath continue to bring awareness to your body . . .

. . .

As you breathe deeply, begin to imagine your breath caressing you,
  allowing your body to feel sensual . . .
Just breathe into your sensuality.
Let your breath caress you with sensuality . . .
Feel your whole body as sensual.
Just let yourself surrender to your sensual feelings . . .
Let out a sound.
Truly experience your sensuality.
How does your body feel?
Luxuriate in the feelings . . .
You are a sensual being.
Enjoy yourself.

Let the feelings begin to become sexual.
Feel the sensuality and sexuality in every part of your body . . .
Let the sexuality come up . . .
Just let it rise within you.
Let it fill you.
Be aware of every part of your body
  and how sensual each might be.
How sexual.
Allow yourself to be in touch with your sexuality . . .
Keep letting it rise.
What images come up?
What or who?
What creates these sexual sensations?
What images do these sensations create?
Surrender to it.
Get a complete sense of your sexual self . . .
  your sexuality vibrating within you . . .
Your sexual energy is vibrating in harmony with all of the other
  energies in your body and with the energy of the earth and uni-
  verse.

Sexual energy is expressing itself in your body.
See the things that arouse these feelings . . .
Bathe in the sensations . . .
Let out a sound.
Begin to feel your whole body being surrounded by a caressing,
soothing mist.

Let the sexual energy run wild in your body.
Let out a sound.
Notice how every part of your body feels.
What are the sensations?
What do you feel like?
Feel the energy in your body.
Your sexual energy.
Breathe and be aware of the vibration.
Be aware of your whole body.
How do you feel about yourself right now?
Take a deep breath.
Let out a sound.

Now begin to listen to your mind, and hear voices off in the mist.
Try to strain to see through the mist.
As it begins to clear, know that what you will begin to see
are times in your life that determined how you really feel
about yourself and sex.

Who is there?
What is happening?
How old are you?
Let the event unfold . . .
Take all the time you need to re-create the experience for yourself.

Allow yourself to have the feelings that you had then . . .
Remember you are in a safe place, these are only memories . . .
Breathe deeply and let out a sound.

What were you told about sex?
Who told you that?
Were you told that it wasn't okay?
If this never happened, then just rest and be with your body.
Otherwise hear what you were told.
How did you feel?
How did you feel about yourself?
Breathe through your body.
Let out a sound.
How did you feel about sex?
What did they tell you?

What happened to you that determined how you feel about your-
  self sexually?
What did you decide?
Let out a sound.
Feel it in your body.
This is where you set up your patterns about yourself sexually.
What are those patterns?
See those patterns.
See them clearly.
Let out a sound.
Be willing to release the patterns so that you have choice,
  so that you can experience joy.
This is a chance to let go of whatever doesn't serve.

Who judged you?
Who hurt you?

What did they do to you?

Who were they?

Who made the rules?

Who set your limits?

Who said you're not all right?

Who said the way you like to have sex is wrong?

Who do you need to talk to in order to experience sexual freedom?

What do you need to say to free yourself?

What did you need to say then?

Speak out now!

Say whatever you need to know that you are a wonderful sexual being and that it is fine with the universe!

Whom do you need to tell?

It might be yourself.

Do it now!

Say whatever you need to say to be released from your sexual patterns.

Let out a sound!

Take all the time that you need to feel free . . .

When you've experienced a release, begin to let that mist surround you once again.

Allow it to take away all of the limits and judgments and rules.

Allow it to take away all of the history that does not allow you to be free.

Feel it caressing and healing you.

Surrender to the mist and to the freedom.

Allow your sensuality to begin to flow again.

Begin to let your sexual energy express itself in your body again.

Let those feelings return.

Welcome them.

Know that they are all right, that you are all right.

Feel the energy flow through your body.

Now begin to let the mist fade and create for yourself a sexual experience that is the best you can imagine.

Remember this is the era of AIDS, so given the need to be safe and to care for your body, allow yourself to have the most wonderful, complete experience.

Feel it in your body.

Let out a sound.

How do you want sex to be?

Surrender your whole body to the feeling . . .

Keep letting go.

How do you feel?

Let yourself have it exactly the way you want it . . .

Safe and self-affirming, powerful, joyous sex.

Sex the way you most exquisitely deserve it . . .

The most wonderful sex that you can imagine . . .

What is it like?

What do you want?

What are you doing?

How do you feel about yourself, free of the past, free of history, free to choose!

Stay in the experience until you feel complete . . .

Begin to allow the experience to fade.

Allow the sensations to stay in your body.

Feel your sexual energy.

Let go of the experience and be aware of your body.

Really be in touch with every inch of your body.

Feel the sexual energy vibrating in your body.

Feel it vibrating around each cell in your body.

Allow this energy to awaken the memory of your sexual self,
before there were rules.

Know that you are a free spirit.

Your sexual energy is part of the natural flow of the energy of
creation.

Feel your body fill with the light of these energies
and just be with yourself for a moment.

Your sexual energy is part of your spiritual expression,
part of the expression of your genuine, powerful, deserving self.

Now you are beginning to break out of the restrictive patterns of your sexual upbringing. These are powerful patterns to break. The feelings you have around your sexuality reach way beyond the direct effect it has on your sexual life into the very fiber of your sense of self. Bringing these sexual feelings into reality and into the present will put you on the path to being able to have fulfilling relationships and being truly intimate with yourself and others.

Relationships and Intimacy

W*hen I saw her, I knew she was everything I wanted. When she smiled I felt good. When we made love I felt like a man. When we fought I knew I was alive. She let me feel and feeling was something I hadn't been doing. When she left I didn't know who I was.*

John Mordaunt, *London, 1987*

RELATIONSHIPS PROVIDE A FERTILE SOIL FOR THE BLOOMING OF YOUR MOST POTENT AND DANGEROUS PATTERNS. The source of your relationship patterns is your parents. Your first relationships in the world are with them, and theirs is the first relationship that you witness and absorb. In effect, your relationship to them and theirs to each other become your unconscious role models for relationships, your root relationships.

Like drugs, or alcohol, or food, your own relationships in their romantic stages can allow you to feel high, to ignore reality, to soothe your pain, need, and loneliness, and can lull you into a false sense of well-being. You hide in romantic relationships. You invest in romantic relationships. If the romance is not grounded in reality, then when the rose glow wears off you will be faced with life and each other under the glaring baldness of fluorescent light.

Unlike substances, relationships ultimately tend to bring up rather than suppress the issues in your life. You look to a relationship to be your salvation and to end the pain of separation from your Genuine Self. You have the mistaken notion that you can fill the void in your heart with someone else or make up for the past in the present. You think if you can effect intimacy with another person, you will make up for your lack of intimacy with yourself. So you run headlong into relationship after relationship without thinking about the ramifications or what it is that you actually want.

You go into them not seeing the people that you are with, but your fantasies, your hopes, and your needs. You go into them trying to fill the gaps left by your childhood, trying to make up for the past in the present. You dump all of the stuff that you need onto *the one*. Is it any wonder that most of your relationships are doomed from the start until you look at the connection between your current relationship and your root relationships?

It is mistakenly said that you keep marrying the same person over and over again. In reality, those people are quite different from one another. Reality will tell us that there are two things that actually are the same. First, you are present in each of the relationships. Second, at some time in the relationship you begin to feel about yourself the way you have in other relationships and in childhood. Your patterns emerge. What you are most often doing is re-creating the unfinished business of the past. The Impostor is so skillful that you are unable to see the patterns. You plunge ahead as if you are actually involved in the present.

When I first met the man who became my husband, I thought I was meeting Prince Charming. He looked like a prince to me. He was Mr. Right. He was very handsome, very charming; a little closed off, but I could fix that; a little preoccupied, but I could get his attention. His description could double as a description of my father, but I was too young and unwise to see that. My Impostor had led me into the mist of romance, illusion, and need. If ignorance creates bliss, I remained blissfully ignorant, ignoring the gnawing sensations of my instincts, bringing them in line with reason. My need was to be needed, to belong, and to be primary to someone. And so I was until the feelings of isolation and longing that I had experienced in childhood surfaced once again. Suddenly, Mr. Right was all wrong.

After a turbulent separation, I went out into the world to find the next relationship to fill the void. My first try out of wedlock looked entirely different. He was a different race, from a different culture. He was an intellectual who allowed my mind to stretch into places it hadn't wandered before. Every moment was an adventure. Then, quite abruptly, be began to seem just like Mr. Right. He couldn't have been more different, and yet he was the same. Or was he? I began to feel choked and isolated and unable to find myself. He began to sound like the first Mr. Right, and though I tried to make myself right for him, everything felt all wrong and I made another spring for freedom. In reality, there wasn't enough caring or loving that he or anyone could have given me to make me feel wanted and to assure me that I deserved a primary place in anyone's life, including my own.

Undaunted, unwise, and unconscious of my patterns from the past, I tried all shapes, sizes, sexes, ethnic backgrounds, intellectual levels, and occupations. And still they were all the same. Or were they?

Actually, what was the same was the fact that I was in each of the relationships, and after the glow of romance wore off I was face-to-face with my unconscious feelings of separation, my longing to be wanted, and my fear of being emotionally abandoned. These were feelings that I have dragged with me throughout my life without being aware of their effect or their origin. These feelings would trigger a hopeless sense that I was always going to feel this way and that no one would ever really love me enough. Once, in a very dramatic relationship-ending scene, I heard myself say as I slammed out the door, "If I wanted to feel like this I would have stayed with my ex-husband or my father! " I said it, but I didn't hear the underlying meaning.

The relationship that I had fled to in order to avoid pain had actually caused me pain. What I had hoped would save me just kept me looking for a lifeline. Relationships will continually present you with unfinished business from the past until you resolve it. If you haven't yet discovered that as an abused or misunderstood or unnurtured child, you were warped away from intimacy, you will keep bringing relationships into your life to mirror your unresolved childhood issues. Until you are able to recognize the core beliefs that separate you from your Genuine Self, you will keep re-creating the experience of those beliefs.

I want to get back to this Prince Charming business for a moment. If you have pictures of what your perfect relationship would be like or have pictures of what the perfect person is like, when you meet someone you will make that person fit your pictures. Alas, illusion is transitory and eventually reality will rear its head. You will usually blame the object of your illusion for not fitting your picture. If you have ever been on the other side of the equation you know that it hurts to discover that you aren't enough, never were, and that in fact you have gone essentially unseen.

In search of a mate to fill the void inside yourself, you may—particularly if you are the codependent type—choose someone whom you are pretty sure won't fit your perfect pictures but whom you think you can fix. You see that person as raw material, potential. How many meals can you eat with potential? How many days and nights can you devote to bringing out the best in the one you are with?

Entanglements are not relationships. They are substitutes for real love and usually require two damaged children who are re-creating their root relationships. For example, an alcoholic and a codependent are both deeply in need of support, help, and sorting out. Neither is the bad guy and neither is the victim. The alcoholic looks like the bad guy because he or she may be getting arrested, driving drunk, being violent, and losing jobs, while the helpmate just serves, and keeps the home fires burning while sacrificing unselfishly. Reality would tell us that the helpmate would rather deal with the alcoholic's issues than his or her own.

As I often see in workshops, women in abusive relationships who are beaten are victimized. It is, however, the need of their childhood training to be the victim. Such people will be naturally attracted to those who will victimize them. Often these relationships begin with romance and the illusion that things are different, but the illusion is soon replaced with abuse. The relationship is replaced with the entanglement of childhood issues. Both parties were probably abused children and are acting out their need to repeat their root relationships in different roles, complimentary roles.

While the Impostor is still in charge of your relationships it may be your pattern to look for what you want from people who cannot give it to you. You will seek affection from those who have trouble expressing it. You will long for intimacy from those who have trouble being intimate. You will look for security from those who can't get their lives together. Then you become their victim and resent them.

You are smart enough not to go to a Chinese restaurant and order Mexican food, making the owner wrong for not having enchiladas! What's the difference? Why is it that you will continually, time after time, look for what isn't there in relationships?

There is a technology to romantic relationships. In the beginning there is the excitement of finding yourself enveloped in the glow of newness. The best qualities of each of you are reflected in the eyes of the other. You wriggle in the rapture of finding things you have in common and discovering the things that you lack, present in the other.

She may be more adventurous than you and so it pushes you to try new things. He may know things about the world that you want to learn.

As the newness of the romance wears off, so does the illusion that you are both just perfect. You begin to see the things you do not like about yourself reflected in your loved one. As the illusion falls away the reality of your life shows up, along with your unresolved past.

When you begin to feel the way you always have, or the situations seem all too familiar, you are being presented with an opportunity to see what patterns are warping your ability to be intimate. What part of the past are you trying to work out? You are being offered a chance to release the Impostor, who is doomed to re-create your root relationships, and embrace your Genuine Self, who is longing for real intimacy.

Relationships are always out of balance unless you can tell the truth about them. If you are not relating to someone in the light of reality and truth you cannot be intimate. You will never have more than the illusion of intimacy.

There are few role models for true intimacy. Your root relationships seldom provide you with an experience of intimacy. In fact, it is most likely that as a small child you learned to shut down, withdraw from intimacy, and withhold your Genuine Self. In order to fit into your family system, you most likely had to start pretending that you were who your mother and father wanted you to be. It was a way to get approval or love. Even if you took a rebellious route you had to withhold parts of yourself to get by. As soon as you begin to withhold parts of yourself or to pretend to be the way others want you to be, intimacy is precluded. Your parents most likely had a relationship with who you pretended to be. They had a relationship with your Impostor. Your Genuine Self was unavailable to them.

This pattern continues as you grow up. You withhold the parts of yourself that you think will be unacceptable. Your survival mechanisms replace your availability and vulnerability. You give your power away to your need to be liked, loved, and accepted.

This need is strongest when you meet someone you are attracted to or fall in love with. You offer the person that you think he or she wants you to be. You offer the qualities that you like about yourself and pretend the rest don't exist. The likelihood is that the person you have the illusion of being in a relationship with is doing the same thing. So what you have is two pretenses having a relationship. Two Impostors pretending to be intimate.

To be truly intimate you need to be fully visible. The things that you like about yourself and things that you don't cannot be hidden. No lies. Your Genuine Self will be available for a relationship with the Genuine Self of another.

In order to walk through life ready for intimacy, there is work to be done. The first thing to do is to look at your root relationships with your parents or primary caretakers. It is necessary to see just exactly who these people were and why they behaved the way they did. They too grew up in dysfunction. It takes awareness to understand that the way you were treated as a child followed naturally on the heels of the way they were treated as children. Given the reality of their lives your experience of growing up was probably a logical consequence.

They followed their role models, or lack of them. They drew on their experience and thought patterns and fears. They probably did the best they could. If you can really discover who these people were and have compassion for them, you can begin to stop the cycle of blame and see that just as they were not to blame, neither are you. Remember, you aren't your behavior or your history!

There is no blame, and there is no going back to right old wrongs. What there is, is a chance to see the relationship with your parents in the light of the truth and begin to let them and yourself off the hook. You can discover the issues that keep you tied to your history and you can begin to see where you have re-created those relationships along the way and in the present. You can see the patterns and break them.

It is important to allow yourself to go back to the time in childhood when you began to withhold intimacy from your parents. You may have done this as a means of survival. You may have had to pretend or cover up who you really were or felt. Let yourself go back. Encounter first one parent, then the other.

I suggest that after that you take a little break and then go back to use the rest of the exercise to examine other relationships in your life that seem unresolved, as well as your present relationships. In this way you can be in reality and be opened to be intimate with all of the people in your life, to be available for intimacy. It is a lot of work but there are great rewards.

*Take a deep breath and reconnect to the energies from the center
of the earth and the vast universe.*
Feel those energies flowing through your body.
*Let the energy surround each cell and let it bring light into your
heart.*
Let it radiate from your heart and through your body.
Let it radiate beyond and fill your field of vision.

See yourself at the center of the light.
Just be with yourself.
Really see yourself.
See an image of yourself reflected in the light.
Look into your own eyes . . .
Let your thoughts go.
Breathe through your body and see how you feel about yourself.
Let out a sound.
*Just be with yourself, your own image, as you breathe peacefully
and deeply.*

*Off in the distance, begin to see an image of your mother (or
father).*
Just be there.
Let out a sound.
Let your mother approach you.
Allow her to come as close to you as is comfortable.
Just be there with your mother.
See those things about you that are like her.
Those traits that you share.
Take a breath and see how you feel about yourself.
Let out a sound.

. . .

*Listen to your thoughts and stay in touch with your feelings as
   you are with your mother.*
How do you feel about yourself when you are with your mother?
How do you feel about her?
Take your time.

Try to see her free of your thoughts and position and expectations.
*Let her tell you who she is and how she came to feel that way
   about herself.*
Where did she get her sense of self?
How has that affected the way she relates to you?
What about her childhood expectations and hopes?
Take plenty of time . . .
Let her tell you what she wants you to know about her.
Just listen . . .
Be with her . . .
Hear her.
Now breathe through your body.
How do you feel?
Just be with your mother and take a deep breath.
*Allow yourself to go back in time to that moment
   when you began to withhold intimacy from her.*
See that time.
Feel it in your body.
How small were you?
What happened?
Who was there?
See the moment when you stopped being honest with your mother.
What did it feel like to be you then?
*When did you shut down and stop expressing yourself to your
   mother?*

What was it that triggered the shutdown?
What closed you off?
Experience it in your body.
See the moment and breathe into the places in your body
 where you feel the shutdown.
Feel the cost.
Let out a sound.
Now begin to breathe life into those places and open up.
Allow yourself to open up.
Risk it! Risk intimacy!
Open up! Open up!
Let out a sound.
It is safe here.
Let those defenses go!
Breathe through them.
Stay open!

What would you have needed to have said when you were little
 to have stayed open and been intimate?
What did you want to say that you didn't or couldn't?
What would you have done?
What did you need then?
Say it now!
Say everything that you wanted to say then, everything that you
 couldn't.
Let the little child speak.
What did you want from her in the moment?
What did you want?
What did you want to know?
Let the child ask.
Let her see you just as you are now.
Let her see who you are.
No blocks, nothing shut down or hidden.

Keep breathing into those places where you experience intimacy
    and just be there with her.

Let her see who you are, who you really are.
Tell her everything that you have ever withheld from her.
Every lie, every need, every hurt, every expectation, resentment,
    wish.
Just go for it.
Don't hold anything back, it's too costly.
Keep breathing and stay open.
Tell her everything about you and how you feel
    that you have been afraid to say.
Say whatever you need to be free.

Now say whatever you need to say to let you both off the hook.
Bring the relationship into the moment, nothing hidden.
Say whatever needs to be said so you can be with each other in
    the present.
This doesn't mean that you need to like each other or approve of
    the way the other lives, it just means that you see each other
    and allow each other to be who you are.

Allow yourselves to be together in the moment, in reality,
    allow judgment to dissolve away.
What does she need to hear from you?
What might she need to hear to be free to be herself with you?
Just say it . . .
Let her say anything else that she might say before you let her go.
Just be with her.
Anything else?
Now is the time to be free and complete.

Is there anything else before you let her go?
Breathe into your body and simply say it.

Be with her and begin to let your images merge.
See those things about you that are alike and
   breathe into the place in your body where your compassion lies.
Allow that compassion to be there for both of you.
Allow that compassion to run through you.
Now allow her image to fade and be there with yourself.
(Repeat for your father, then take a little break. When you come
   back to work reconnect to the energies and . . .)

Take a deep breath and see how you feel about yourself in this
   moment.
See yourself standing in the middle of a great circle of light.
In that light begin to see all of the people in your life
   with whom you are in relationships.
Intimate, business, casual, present, past, living, dead.
Let whoever appears be there, even if it doesn't make sense.
They are there for a reason.
Don't force anyone to be there.

Look at each person in this circle.
Take your time and gaze at them one by one.
As you look at each of them, breathe through your body.
See how you feel about yourself with them.
How do you feel about them?
Look into their eyes . . .
What is the relationship?
Not what you might wish it to be or pretend that it is, but how it
   is in reality.

Is it the way you want it?
See yourself with them . . .
What is it like?
Take a breath and let out a sound.
When you know all that you need to know for the moment,
   go on to the next person.
Just a brief glance may be all you need for now.
A glance and a breath.
Let the relationship that most urgently needs to be completed come
   forward.
Be with that person and see them clearly.
Be with them, breathe through your body and see
   how you feel about yourself when you are with that person.
Let out a sound.
How do you feel about them?
See what it might be about you that is like them.
How does that feel?

See the relationship the way it really is . . .
See the truth . . .
Be honest with yourself . . .
How does that feel?
Let out a sound.
Let any illusions and pretenses fall away . . .
Be with the relationship in reality, in the moment.
Not your pictures or how you wanted it, or the way is was sup-
   posed to be, or used to be. (Take your time.)
Let go of the illusions; they keep you from being intimate.
Just be with them.
See if you pierce through your needs, your perceptions,
   your disappointments or expectations and just see who they are.
Let them tell you who they are.
Allow them to tell you about how it was for them to grow up.

Allow them to tell you the truth about how it has been for them.
Let them tell you what their hopes and dreams were.
Let them tell you how it feels to be them . . .
Their expectations and disappointments.
Hear them tell you who they think they are.
See their separation from their Genuine Selves.

As you allow yourself to be with them,
    go back to where you began to shut down in this relationship.
When did you begin to withhold your intimacy,
    to edit who you are or what you say and feel?
What were you hiding?
What were you afraid of?
What did you really want?
How does that feel in your body?
Let out a sound.
Just see yourself at the moment that you began to withhold your-
    self and breathe through your body.
Let out a sound.
Allow yourself to re-create the experience in your body.
See yourself at that time.
What was happening?
Why did you shut down?
What did you withhold?
How did it feel in your body?
What was it that you wanted?
What was it that you really wanted to say?
Now is the time to allow yourself to say these things,
    to say what you really wanted.
See what you were afraid of and see that shutting down
    and being silent have been very costly.
Breathe through your body and the shutdown and let yourself say
    everything that you wanted to say then.

Say everything you would have needed to say to tell the truth,
    to express yourself, to be free!
Say it all now so that you have have an experience of intimacy.
When you have said everything that you need to say,
    begin to allow the two of you to come into the present.

Be with that person.
What do you need to say or do to be complete, to be present?
If there is anything you have been withholding, say it now.
It's safe.
Tell them everything you've been afraid to say, afraid they'd
    find out.
What have you wanted to ask?
Leave nothing hidden.
Risk it!
Say it all!
The cost of holding on is too great!
Say everything that you have ever withheld.
Tell them how you have wanted it, what you've needed,
    who you've made them out to be.
See if there is anything else that you need to let go of and just let
    it go.
    (Take your time).

Let the person see you.
All of you, just as you are.
Be there with them.
Breathe.
See how it feels.
Let them be with you.
See if you can see who they are now.
See who they really are, not who you've needed or invented.

Just who they are.
Their reality.
What does it feel like?
If there's fear or thoughts or resistance let it go.
This is what it feels like to relate, human to human.
Intimate.
Just be with each other.
What do you reflect to each other?
Breathe into your compassion and wrap yourself in it.
See if there is anything else that you want to say to be complete
and open and free before you let them go.
Say it now.
When you feel a release let them fade and come back to your
space, bringing with you the sensations of intimacy.

What you have just done is allow yourself an experience of openness and the possibility of intimacy. Intimacy is the thing you fear most and—at the same time—most long for. Before you can experience intimacy, you need to tell the truth and free yourself of the patterns you run in relationships and the patterns you run in other areas of your life. In this way you can begin to experience yourself as whole. The only place you can ever expect to feel whole is within yourself. I don't mean to say that until you are whole you cannot have wonderful relationships. What you can have is relationships that are what they are, and with the people they are with. You can see who people really are, and on that basis you can choose to be with them, or not. Choice is powerful and fulfilling.

If you are not intimate with yourself, if you do not nurture yourself, if you do not love yourself, you will still feel the separation from your Genuine Self. Two people genuinely working on their own well-being and on intimacy can work together. It is all possible to do; it just takes compassion, commitment, and the truth.

Being Intimate with Yourself

So! If I just can remember who I am, then the whole world opens up to me! Since I don't always remember, I decided to keep people around me who never let me forget.

Ted Karavidas, *New York, 1990*

As OUT OF HARMONY AS YOU MAY HAVE BEEN WITH THE WORLD AROUND YOU, IT HAS TAKEN ALL OF THIS PREPARATION TO COME FULL CIRCLE TO THE POINT OF ALLOWING YOURSELF TO BE INTIMATE WITH YOUR GENUINE SELF. As hidden as you have been from others, that is how hidden you have been from yourself. Since the system has needed to stay in place and the Impostor has needed to live your life for you, it has been necessary that you be distant from your Genuine Self. When you are intimate with yourself you can see through the veil of amnesia and recognize who you are on the deepest level. Once you see yourself through the loving eyes of intimacy, you can no longer experience yourself the way the Impostor intended you to.

Intimacy with yourself is the point from which you can step out into the world and have an effect on it. Once you can clearly see your Geniune Self, and grow intimate with yourself, you can have an impact on the world that is a reflection of principles rather than dysfunctional need.

In order to regain the self-intimacy that you were born with, I'm going to ask you to go back in time. In your life, long ago, there was a moment when you began to withdraw, to withhold, to shut down, and to create a pretense to represent you in the world, and to yourself. In other words, you began to withhold intimacy from yourself in the way you withhold it from others.

What follows is a visualization very much like the one in which you looked at resolving your relationships with others. In this process you will resolve your relationship with yourself and embrace your Geniune Self, enabling you to move fully into life.

In order to do this, you will retrace your steps back to the original moments of separation from yourself. You will begin to see what happened, or to get as close to it as you can. The child that you were remembers, so you will go back to your childhood and investigate the source of your separation, and look boldly at the times when you began to withhold intimacy from yourself and began to pretend that you were less than wonderful. When was it you decided that survival was dependent on withholding intimacy?

Once again, do all of the things that you need to
   to get yourself ready for the journey back to your true self.
Reconnect to the energies from the earth.
Reconnect to the energies from the infinite universe.
Breathe all of that wonderful energy into your body.
Allow them all to radiate through you in the form of light.
Let the light radiate through you and beyond, filling your field of
   vision.

See how you feel about getting to know who you are
   and reuniting in the harmony that was meant to be.
In the light, let an image of yourself appear.
Just be with yourself.
Look into your own eyes.
Let out a sound.
Be there with yourself and breathe through your body . . .

Allow yourself to begin to go back in time.
Go back in time to when you were very, very small.
Allow an image to appear of when you were little.
Let your body feel little and vulnerable.
See if you can go to a time when you began to withdraw from
   yourself.
When did you begin to withhold intimacy from yourself?

When did you begin to pretend to be less than you are?
Less powerful?
Less deserving?
Less loving?
When did you begin to shield your vulnerability?

Let yourself re-create that time.
What was happening?
How old were you?
Let your little body feel what it was like.
Who was there?
What was happening?
Let the events unfold moment by moment.
See the real moments, just the facts. What did it feel like?
Who was with you?
What did you decide?
When did you shut down?
Feel the shutdown in your little body.
Feel the pretense, the loss of intimacy.
Feel the cost.
See yourself.
Experience yourself as if you were there.
Let your whole body feel the experience.
Let out a sound.
See the moment.
Who was there?
What happened?
When was it?
Feel yourself there.
How do you feel about yourself?
Let the moments unfold and feel them in your body . . .
What were you thinking?

*What rules did you make up about yourself and the way the world
is?*

What did you cast in stone that day?

*What decisions did you make about the way it would always or
never be?*

Take your time . . .

This is the beginning of many patterns, many themes.

This is a moment that had great importance.

Feel it . . .

What did the little child really want and need?

Say the words to yourself now.

Take all the time you wanted . . .

Just say what you really wanted to say.

Ask for what you really needed.

What might it have felt like to get what you wanted?

*To be allowed to feel your power, that you were deserving and
lovable?*

*Breathe into that place of compassion and let the child speak to
you for a moment.*

Give yourself what the little child wanted.

Let yourself feel what it feels like.

Feel the love the child needed.

Know that it is real and that you have it for yourself.

*Breathe deeply into the places in your body where you feel love
and allow that sensation to bathe you in love.*

Be with your child self until you feel safe and in harmony.

Then, keeping those feelings, move into the present.

Allow the feelings of love and harmony and safety to remain.

Be there with your own image.

Just see yourself as you really are, no pretense left.

No separation.

Just your Genuine Self.

Look into your eyes.

Be with yourself and keep breathing.

Breathe into the compassion that you have and surround yourself with it.

Know that it is safe to be yourself, your true, powerful, deserving self.

Look deeply into your adult self.

What do you need to say to yourself to feel a release?

To be intimate with yourself?

What have you been longing to hear?

Set yourself free.

Free of the history that has kept you from being intimate with yourself.

Free to be intimate with others.

Free of the Impostor.

Free of the Impostor that served you well and allowed you to survive.

Free of survival.

Free to live in the rapturous experience of full expression and self.

Allow your image to fill with light.

The light of the truth.

Feel the light in your own body.

Know that this light is a reflection of your Genuine Self.

A reflection of your Genuine Self.

This light is who you are, a radiant reflection of a human being.

A human being having human experiences.

Begin to allow yourself to see your life as an endless world of possibilities.

Know that when you are intimate with yourself you know your worth and can create a life of joy and fulfillment.

> *In this life you will also be able to have all of the experiences*
>   *of being human without interrupting that flow of self-love.*
> *Let yourself fully experience this state.*
> *When you are ready, come back into awareness of the room*
>   *around you.*
> *When you are able, go to the mirror.*
> *Just be there with yourself, looking into your eyes.*
> *Be with yourself for at least five minutes.*
> *After five minutes sit quietly and write yourself a love letter.*
> *Write yourself a love letter that says everything you've been long-*
>   *ing to hear.*
> *Let it pour from your heart and your Genuine Self.*
> *Don't edit or think about it.*
> *Write all of the things that you have known in your heart*
>   *but were unable to reach through the veil of amnesia.*
> *Let yourself know the truth about your own grace*
>   *and let yourself know what you really want and need in your*
>   *life.*
> *Trust that you can create a world that will reflect your Genuine*
>   *Self.*

Once you know that you are truly powerful, wonderful, and deserving, you are free from the addiction to the past. Once you've experienced yourself, you have broken the addictive cycle. Once you have opened your arms to your Genuine Self, you are free to accept the support that it takes to stay intimate with yourself; you are free to have your feelings, have intimate relationships, make mistakes, have what you desire, look at reality and truth, and forge a life that works for you, embracing a personal vision for a greater reality. You are ready to move on to Life Mastery.

Life Mastery

Life Mastery

I *am completely amazed at the changes in my life. Some-how I was blessed enough to begin to waltz to my own tune. I'd danced everyone else's dance and it didn't work. Ultimately I learned to turn it all over to a higher power. I don't understand it and I don't need to understand it. It just works.*

Steven Bradley, *Houston, 1990*

AS YOU LEARN TO MASTER LIVING, YOU WILL CREATE IN YOURSELF THE SAFETY TO TRAVEL INTO THE UNKNOWN, WHERE YOUR BRILLIANCE AND FREEDOM LIE. In order to do this you may find yourself doing some things and behaving in ways that feel completely unreasonable.

Does it seem unreasonable to give up survival? Does it seem unreasonable to let go of the restrictive concepts and rigid systems that have gotten you this far? Does it seem unreasonable to let go of your ego and will? Does it seem unreasonable to embrace your spiritual source? Does it seem unreasonable to live life passionately? Does it seem unreasonable to embrace your personal vision and participate in shaping the world that you live in?

This kind of unreasonableness leads to Life Mastery and to what I call Whole Living. Whole Living is the antithesis of living in a malfunctioning system. Whole Living is the result of the work it takes to allow your history to be behind you, to live in reality, and to look to a future that is free of habitual behavior, abuse, denial, and dysfunction. Whole Living allows you to express your genuine self.

This section of *Life Mastery* is a call to move beyond the specter of reason into the world of the unexplored and the unrestricted. Unreasonable people transcend the limitations of the systems that they grow up within. It is people who have been unreasonable who have changed the face of society. It is people who are unreasonable who can hold on to their visions in the face of "the way it's always been." It was the unreasonableness of the Impressionists who changed the way we perceive art for all time, and the unreasonableness of Jackson Pollock and his colleagues that shifted our vision once more. The same quality of unreasonableness has changed music, theater, science, and medicine. Whole Living requires the ability to see the world through new eyes. Whole Living takes a vision and a willingness to see to it that your vision has form.

I once had the privilege of spending a day in the studio of Christo, the artist who is responsible for pushing the outside of the envelope in the world of conceptual and environmental art. In the face of narrow minds, meagerly creative governments, and a bewildered and often hostile public, he has wrapped buildings and the Pont Neuf in Paris, and draped tons of fabric across the Great Gorge in a piece of art called *The Valley Curtain.* His *Surrounded Islands* off the coast of Florida were just that, islands that were surrounded by a special brilliant pink waterproof fabric, and he created the *Running Fence,* a graceful fabric wall undulating in the wind across twenty-six miles of Northern California sheep farms. Being in the presence of people such as Christo, who are willing to follow their vision and enrich their own lives and the lives of others because they have transcended limitations—that is an inspiration.

You can live out of this consciousness.

Music, literature, science, politics, society, and your own life can be shifted by acts of unreasonableness. In the face of the way the system is set up, it is unreasonable to thrive and to live in joyous, productive rapture. Yet it can be done.

One way that you can be unreasonable is to live life fully, embracing and expressing your Genuine Self and holding your personal vision and worldview in the face of the way it has always been for you. You can take what you have discovered about your personal life and apply it to the systems in which you live—to societal, national, and global systems.

The dysfunction of the family is replayed throughout all levels of society. The family system is a microcosm of the systems that you inherit from society. The church, the state, the federal government, the global network are all deeply dysfunctional. The primary function of these systems is to perpetuate themselves.

It is unclear whether the dysfunction of global society is a reflection of the dysfunctional family or vice versa. It is a sort of chicken-or-egg conundrum, and ultimately it doesn't matter. What matters is that we stop the addictive cycle of dysfunction in society, religion, government, the global family, and the personal family. If you are unreasonable enough, you can shift the way life is experienced by humankind for all time as you continue to live as a Life Master.

Real Spirituality

I have long believed, and consistently said, that in all things there is divine purpose. I do not pretend to understand God's ways, but I believe that even my being HIV-positive is within the divine plan. And I draw comfort from that.

Mary Fisher, *Boca Raton, 1992*

IF YOU WANT TO REEMBRACE YOUR GENUINE SELF, EMBRACE WHOLE LIVING, AND HAVE AN IMPACT ON SOCIETY, YOU WILL BE GREATLY ENRICHED AND SUPPORTED BY GETTING IN TOUCH WITH YOUR SPIRITUAL SOURCE. But what if your concept of spirit has been muffled by a constricting idea of God?

You will need to trust a force or power greater than your ego or intellect; that power is your Spiritual Source. The form is not important, and preoccupation with the form of spirituality—or whatever you call it, for that matter—can lead you back into the constrictions of a new or old religion. If the form is not important, even an atheist can be connected to a Spiritual Source. Perhaps for an atheist it might be called creativity or intuition. The point is that when people have tapped into their creativity or the real needs of others, they have transcended their egos and their minds.

As you grow up, your concept of spirituality becomes very muddled. You are taught to believe in the God invented by the system. God is used in abusive ways to frighten children into a particular morality and behavior. That is spiritual abuse. It is abusive to threaten a child with eternal damnation. It is abusive to lie to a kid about what God sees and doesn't see, what God cares about and doesn't care about, and what God does to bad little girls and boys. It is abusive for adults to get their way by invoking the fear of God. Fearing God does not mean you are good, it means that you are afraid. Fearing God does not mean anything but the presence of spiritual abuse.

When people tell you what "God says," they are using God to make their own point. It is bad enough that ministers, both fundamentalist and New Age, do this to adults, but to do it to a child is a transgression and makes it hard for a child to trust or to truly love God.

Children have a brilliant connection to their spiritual natures. Left to themselves they could create a relationship with spirituality that grew from their own conscience and wonder at the world around them. If God were put in a loving context as they grew up, they might continue to connect the idea of love with spirit. They might still equate their own creativity with creation.

When I was a kid, I remember trying to figure out how to be good. God always seemed to be pissed off. The more I was told about God the more afraid of God I became. After all, we are talking about someone who turned a woman into a pillar of salt just for looking over her shoulder. I even got a little confused between God and Santa Claus. I knew that they both could see me when I was sleeping and awake and that they both knew if I'd been bad or good.

As I got older and picked up some political awareness, I noticed that some white people in the South (I didn't notice it in my own neighborhood) said God wanted to keep the schools segregated and keep black people in the back of the bus. I gathered that some people in the Middle East declared that God had set a parcel of land aside for them and they could just move right in over the objections of the people who had been there for generations. I saw pictures of the starvation in the world and began to read a history that was laden with hatred and prejudice labeled morality and the will of God. Before I knew what one was, I became an atheist. The concept of God that I was being taught on all fronts was so alien to my personal experience that I denied my experience and I denied God.

It is strange to think of how much control those claiming to speak for God can exercise. In working with clients over the years, I have heard amazing stories of the suffering of children at the hands of nuns in schools where corporal punishment is looked upon as the right of the church, as are humiliation and threats of eternal damnation. There are also the stories that pour from men who went to seminary schools and had their first homosexual experiences with those brothers who teach righteousness, or with choirmasters who also teach them to sing the praises of the God they are taught to fear. That is no relationship with spirit.

Some of these painful and pervasive religious experiences follow us to our deaths. I went to New York to do an AIDS Mastery Workshop and while I was there I was asked to go visit a man named Warren, who was dying in the hospital. Warren had been through our programs. His body had quit, yet he seemed unable to die, to let go. Everyone was trying to figure out what was keeping him. What was Warren waiting for?

I went to see him. He was exhausted. We talked for hours. We looked at the spirituality that he had sought over many years. He wasn't afraid to die. Or at least he didn't think he was. For some reason I asked him what religion he'd been born into. He said that he had been raised Catholic, but that he hadn't practiced that religion for thirty years. Then suddenly he began to cry. He wept bitter tears and said that he just realized how deeply the fear of damnation was ingrained in him. He was a homosexual and he was afraid that he would burn in hell for eternity. Though he knew better, this childhood fear gripped him. What Warren was waiting for was absolution. I left matters in the hands of a young Jesuit who assured me that he would find a compassionate priest to release Warren from the shackles of his rediscovered guilt and fear. The priest released him from his fear of damnation by forgiving him for his perceived fears and invoking God's blessing in a ritual that made Warren happy. Thus he found his absolution and was able to die in relative peace.

With this information I went to Los Angeles, where one of my most brilliant friends, Colin Higgins, the creator of *Harold and Maude, Nine to Five,* and many other classic comedy films, was in the last stages of AIDS. Colin had experienced much shame with his disease and discomfort with his homosexuality. He was having a great deal of trouble accepting his illness. Colin had been on a spiritual quest for years. He knew every guru, mystic, channeler, and soothsayer in the world. He had explored every concept that seemed to offer wholeness. He had pursued cures for AIDS with the same vigor, but at last he had begun to lose his battle with the disease. He also seemed to be losing his spirituality.

Mindful of what had happened with Warren, I broached the subject of shame, guilt, and Catholicism with him. He said that he would like to talk with a priest. Through other people with AIDS I had met a wonderful, warm, and gentle priest who knew and understood the complicated emotional spiritual issues around AIDS. He came to see Colin. Colin asked him if it would be possible to be forgiven. The priest said that Colin had done nothing to be forgiven for, but asked that Colin forgive the church. He explained that mother church had not been good to her child. Mother had turned her back on her child. Her child felt rejected and unloved. He said that the job of the church is to embrace its children and that had not happened. This lifted all of the onus from Colin. He understood that God had love for Colin. Colin now had the release he needed to reconnect with his Genuine Self and his true Spiritual Source, and this allowed him to die feeling accepted by God and a church he thought he had left behind long ago. He found peace and serenity. Would that this priest's compassion and insight were the stand of the church and not just the voice of a unique humanitarian.

My own return to spirituality was less dramatic. I remained an atheist until about twenty years ago. I was on a white-water rafting trip on the Colorado River. The canyons that the river snaked through were the most wonderful paintings I'd ever seen, with brilliant and pale colors, majestic monuments, explosions of sky. I was being seized by a feeling that I had not felt in years, recalling bits and pieces of a sweet sense of childhood, a connectedness I had felt when I was little and playing with what my mother called imaginary friends. Then we hit white water and I forgot everything.

That night we camped on the bank of the river. I slept in a sleeping bag outside the tent. As dawn cracked I opened my eyes and looked up at the canyon as the light rose. The grandeur and the scale and the beauty overwhelmed me. My whole body tingled and I felt as if I were being caressed by a thousand angel wings. The sheer magnitude of what I beheld defied explanation. I understand erosion and glacial movement, how this beauty came to occur. But that is not what I beheld.

What I was seeing was nature. What I saw and experienced was the overwhelming beauty of creation, every nuance a creation of some power beyond my comprehension. In that moment I understood what

God was for me. This was God. This was spirit. This was nature. This came from a source that my finite mind could not grasp. It was my resurrection.

I suddenly realized that it wasn't God I had rejected, it was man's use of God's name. It wasn't God but religion that I had really wanted to separate from. The joy of being reunited with my spiritual self, my Spiritual Source, was so powerful that I spent the entire day weeping. Except when we'd hit the white water. Then I'd say a little prayer. The first in a very long time.

I have been freed by understanding that there is an infinite power that is beyond the grasp of my finite mind. In order to achieve recovery, empowerment, and well-being, it is essential to be free of the rigid rules and limiting systems that produce guilt and failure. This is why I want to restate that New Age religion is not always more free than that ol'-time religion. What I mean by God or Spiritual Source is your personal relationship with spirit. You can't get it from a book or a system or a guru. You can't do God someone else's way. You can learn from others what works for them and take for yourself what resonates within you. Only you can experience it—and when you are in harmony with it, it will begin to express itself. And as it does, you will be in harmony with your Genuine Self.

When you turn yourself over to this power you become cocreative. You do not become dominated by or subservient to or afraid of that power. By recognizing that you are not in *control* of your life and turning matters over to a higher energy and allowing your Spiritual Source to guide you, you can then truly become creative and participate in your growth and your experience of who you are—which is the definition of Mastery.

Whole Living

I *can't tell you what a difference all of this makes. Knowing who I am makes it possible for me to create an environment that is amazing. I guess you'd call it an environment that reflects my self-worth.*

Adam Swanson, *Los Angeles, 1990*

A FUNCTIONAL ENVIRONMENT IS A WHOLE ENVIRONMENT. A whole environment is one in which the truth prevails. Certainly problems continue to exist in this environment, but they do not become the featured players in your life. They are recognized, discussed, and dealt with in an open, caring manner. This is a world where you can honor humanness, and that means honor your imperfections and differences.

In a whole environment, you treat yourself and everyone in your life with the respect that other humans deserve. You offer to yourself and others the stuff that you longed for as a child. What this mostly involves is permission. Permission to be who you really are. Permission to have and express your feelings, and freedom to live without the fear of abuse or reprisals. Permission to have your own perceptions, opinions, and worldview. Permission to be different and unique and spontaneous. Permission to stop living the life that was set out for you by your history. Ultimately this permission comes from you, yourself. Once you have permission you will accept nothing less than a full life. It is what I call Whole Living, the magazine and the New Age notwithstanding.

I'm going to provide you with a list of attributes of Whole Living that I use in many of the workshops I do. It is a compilation of essential qualities that I have gathered from many sources. It can be a powerful guide and useful tool.

Whole Living

1) Your uniqueness and creativity are honored, and so is your spontaneity.

2) Your emotions are honored, and recognized. You are allowed to express them freely.

3) You can tell the truth and can give others the same privilege. You have the freedom to have your own thoughts, perceptions, and opinions: they may not reflect the thoughts and attitudes of others, but it is all right. You don't need everyone to agree with you to earn love or a place in the system. You're not threatened, or if you are, you can say so.

4) You understand that you cannot control the life around you, and you feel your personal power without concealing your vulnerability.

5) Boundaries are honored: there is a powerful sense of self that you never submerge in the issues of others. Your boundaries are respected and your roles are clear and flexible.

6) You can make mistakes, learn from them, and move on without altering your sense of yourself.

7) You are accountable for your words and actions and you know the difference between accountability and blame, as do those around you. You are responsible for your own feelings and for your word, as well as your communication.

8) You are free to be fully yourself and available for intimacy.

And what goes for you goes for everyone. Can you just imagine what might be possible if you lived every day powerfully in the manner outlined above? Well, do that.

I want to be clear that when you are powerful you are also vulnerable. When you are living in the truth, all aspects of yourself are present. Whole Living includes all facets of your personality, the traits you like and those that you don't, with plenty of room to grow. It also contains the need for support and love. These needs are an expression of your vulnerability. You are not meant to be able to "go it alone." You are created to be a social, interactive being. In your vulnerability lies your accessibility. This vulnerability allows others to contribute to your growth and to be intimate with you. You never need to be more powerful than someone else. You never need to re-create the false sense of power that you may have created in order to survive. Together, true power and vulnerability represent wholeness.

When you live your life in wholeness, you are truly available for intimacy. You don't have to withhold or create a pretense, and you are available to be intimate with anyone who is available for intimacy. You never have to alter who you are or what you present, so you give a lot of permission to others to do the same thing. In this way you do not save your "true" self for "the one" person that you hope to find and fall in love with. You *always* represent your "true" self and don't have to place the burden of that freedom on someone else. You simply are available for intimacy, and so when "the one" comes along, she or he will be a wonderful addition to your already whole life, an enrichment to an already rich journey. You can spend more time with "the one," and go deeper than with others, but the quality of *all* the relationships in your life will reflect the quality of your relationship to yourself.

When you live in wholeness you remember all of the things that you wanted as a child. You must keep in mind that you cannot make up for the things that you lacked in the past, but that you can have a very rich present. It is important at the times when childhood feelings appear to give yourself a moment or two to breathe deeply through your body and experience those feelings. When the feelings of the child are there, ask yourself what it is that you want. What do you need, right here, right now? If it is possible to do so, give it to yourself. If not, honor the childhood feelings. They are real and they are crying for your attention. Speak lovingly to yourself, the way you longed to be spoken to. Understand and embrace yourself. In this way you will begin to do this automatically and the childish feelings can slip away so that you can grow up in safety.

Once you feel whole, you can help actual children live whole lives. Thus you can avoid creating yet another generation in the image of malfunction. It is possible to support children who are growing up in deeply dysfunctional families in having a functional relationship with you and others. If you can be a witness for them so that they know that what they experience is valid, they will not have to live in denial. They may have to live a pretense in order to survive, but they won't have to lie to themselves or to you. You can create safety for them and a role model for what is possible. In this way they will have an experience of telling the truth. This may ultimately pave the way for them to feel whole.

It is never too late for Whole Living. You can begin the process at any point in your life. Once you start telling the truth, you can shift the entire nature of life to one of wholeness. Suddenly the people and circumstances that you attract into your life are supportive of your well-being and a brilliant reflection of the possibilities present in a truly functional world. Once you begin to live in wholeness, it becomes so second nature to you that you no longer spend time at it. It is as natural as breathing. As the things you discover move from thought to experience, the shift happens. As the cerebral process is replaced by the visceral assimilation, as breath replaces resistance, as being present replaces thinking about what is going on, the shift occurs.

You are no longer at the mercy of your history and you are no longer willing to view the world as powerless to effect change. If you can shift, so can mankind. If you can move beyond dysfunction, so can the world.

Twelve Steps to Whole Living

One thing I know for sure is that my life is very rich because of recovery. The courage I see around me and the willingness to just be out there with all our feelings inspires me all the time.

Peter Simmons, *Santa Fe, 1992*

YOU HAVE ALREADY ENCOUNTERED MANY OF THE TWELVE-STEP PRINCIPLES THROUGHOUT THIS BOOK. Because of their universality, many of those principles had been a guiding force in my work before I ever read the steps. Like the work that I was doing, the steps present no dogma and demand no self-effacing devotion. There are no stars. No one tells you what to do. It is a program of guidance and discovery.

Within this program I have found the best opportunity for a recovery free of the pitfalls of following a designated leader or a rigid philosophy. I know that it is possible to turn the Twelve Steps into rules and your sponsor into your guru if you are truly not ready. The difference between the program and many of the other recovery systems that we have talked about is that dysfunction is not built into it. You have to put it in. Self-perpetuation is not built into the system so that you need a guru to help you run your life.

In these programs, in order to keep sober or clean or whatever else you want to keep, you need to keep working the principles and coming to meetings. There is evidence that the unconditional support and camaraderie of those who've had similar experiences works on a deep level. The other evidence that the program works is that there is no PR, no hype, no leader, no fund-raisers, and yet it is everywhere. Word of mouth and word of its success have been responsible for this expansion.

The Twelve Steps are simple: they include knowing that you are powerless over the substances or behavior damaging you, that your life is pretty much out of control, that turning things over to a higher power can bring sanity, and that it is vital to be willing to dig into your past and share your ugly secrets as you stay current with the relationships in your life. The steps should be followed more or less in order, usually with the guidance of a sponsor, someone who has been down the same path and can support you.

Some may recoil at the use of rather archaic language. Remember that these steps were created in 1939, a time when things were very different. The steps present a very clear and simple guide, though working them is not always so easy.

The Twelve Steps

(These are taken from AA
and vary slightly by program)

1) We admitted we were powerless over alcohol—that our lives had become unmanageable.
2) Came to believe that a Power greater than ourselves could restore us to sanity.
3) Made a decision to turn our will and our lives over to the care of God *as we understood him.*
4) Made a searching and fearless moral inventory of ourselves.
5) Admitted to God, to ourselves, and to another human being the exact nature of our wrongs.
6) Were entirely ready to have God remove all these defects of character.
7) Humbly asked Him to remove our shortcomings.
8) Made a list of all persons we had harmed, and became willing to make amends to them all.
9) Made direct amends to such people wherever possible, except when to do so would injure them or others.
10) Continued to take a personal inventory and when we were wrong promptly admitted it.
11) Sought through prayer and meditation to improve our conscious contact with God *as we understood Him,* praying only for knowledge of His will for us and the power to carry that out.

12) Having had a spiritual awakening as a result of these Steps, we tried to carry this message to alcoholics, and to practice these principles in all our affairs.

You may already be familiar with the Twelve Steps. If you are unfamiliar with them, you will see that they present a blueprint for Whole Living that is very compatible with the work you've been exploring in this book. They are carved out of the need for recovery from dysfunction. I offer them because they are *one* way to pursue Life Mastery with the fewest pitfalls for the Impostor to use to trick you. Not only are they a good blueprint for individuals, but they are also a wonderful set of guidelines for society. We will look into this notion further, later on.

Please remember when you work the Twelve Steps or the principles in *Life Mastery* that the real addiction that you are after lies deep beneath specific substance abuses and compulsive behaviors. Once your Genuine Self emerges there lies before you a chance to have a very wonderful relationship with yourself and with the world.

Mastery on a Grander Scale

There isn't anything that I have had to deal with around the governmental bureaucracy that I didn't deal with in childhood. It's all the same. Everybody is pretending. Everybody is out for themselves. Nobody seems to grasp the bigger picture or have a long-term worldview. Maybe nobody really cares. I hope that's not the case. I hope I'm just being cynical.

Gabe Kruks, *Los Angeles, 1989*

IF YOU APPLY THE SAME ANALYSIS TO THE GLOBAL COMMUNITY THAT YOU HAVE TO THE PERSONAL FAMILY, YOU WILL SEE THAT THE SAME MALFUNCTIONING SYSTEM IS OPERATIVE. Nations act like members of a dysfunctional family. They invade each other's boundaries. They impose their will over one another. They pretend they are doing it for the other's own good. Lies, acceptance of abuse, denial, and fear are used to cover it all up. Mere survival, rather than well-being, is the name of the game, just as it is for individuals.

Greed, control, image, and the lust for power are all-consuming factors for many institutions, industries, and governments. Pollution, starvation, crime, drugs, war, the irresponsible attitudes toward nuclear weaponry and energy—all of these are manifestations of this dysfunction, reflected on a national and global scale.

Few acts of benevolence or caring transpire between nations. Nor is integrity often a motivation for international interaction, though lip service to integrity is used for the purposes of public relations. Secrecy is an international pastime.

On a personal level, you have discovered that in order to allow your Genuine Self to replace the Impostor that has lived your drama for you, you have had to look at your dysfunction and tell the truth about it. You have had to pierce through the veil of denial and amnesia and expose your deepest flaws to the light of day. Only in this way can you live a functional, rich, whole life.

What has freed you can free every society, every nation. If America is going to heal, if it is going to replace its National Impostor with a Genuine America, then we as a nation will have to look at our dysfunction and tell the truth about it, pierce through our national denial and amnesia, and expose our deepest flaws to the light of day. Only then can America live the functional, rich, whole dream it has promised since its creation.

America will have to admit that it needs recovery.

Once this admission is made—and this must come from the highest levels of government in a way that generates understanding and cooperation—Americans will have to face the truth about this history and the current status of the country. Then America can move on to a functional future. And as with personal recovery and growth, there are many illusions. As with with your personal recovery, the payoff is Whole Living and Life Mastery, this time on a grand scale.

If America went into a real recovery program it could follow the Twelve Steps. The first step of Alcoholics Anonymous would require America to admit that it was powerless—not over alcohol, but its addiction to power and image and righteousness and greed. To follow the second step, America would have to admit that there is a power greater than itself. By doing this we would cease to see ourselves as an omnipotent power with the right and obligation to be a global force, because we would know that there was a greater natural force impelling us toward real right action.

The third step asks us to turn our will and our lives over to a God of our understanding. If there is a power greater than America, a Spiritual Source, then we can relinquish the need for supremacy, and demonstrate acceptance, grace, and humility. In other words, the nation would give up its delusions of grandeur and illusions of control. We would also have to allow that this Spiritual Source was of each citizen's understanding, not a tool of the state.

If America is to recover, it will have to look into the past and tell the truth about it. This would be like doing a "fearless moral inventory of ourselves," as suggested in the fourth step. The fifth step would have us "Admit to God, to ourselves, and to another . . . the exact nature of these wrongs." Now we could begin to tell the truth about our history.

We would have to look at our history of making war, suppressing the rights of people who threaten the status quo, and polluting the environment if it makes money for those who run the system—and we would have to tell the truth about the legacy that we are leaving to our children.

The sixth and seventh steps would have us become ready to give up our defects (which have become habitual and repeat themselves throughout our history) and to ask the God of our understanding to remove these shortcomings. This would mean that we were willing to create a new way to operate as a nation.

The eighth and ninth steps would have us make a list of all the people—and in this case, nations, the environment, Native Americans, political systems, and so on—that we have harmed as a nation, and become willing to make amends to (and for) them all, where possible. In order to make environmental amends, for instance, we would have to admit to each nation that we had stripped of its natural resources and whose air quality we had destroyed that we had done so. We would then need to apologize, stop those actions, and begin to change the way we interact with that nation. We could tell the truth to the citizens who suffer at Three Mile Island, fully exposing the reality of the situation, care for those who have been mortally damaged, where possible, and do what we can to ease the pain of those who suffer.

The tenth step would guide us to take inventory continually so that as we make mistakes they can be admitted and used as lessons, so that national life can go on free of ties to the past.

The eleventh step would keep us in constant contact with that Spiritual Source and continue to guide us to live by good will, not willfulness. It would forever keep us mindful that there is a power greater than America.

The twelfth step would then have America as a nation and Americans as individuals practice these principles in all of our daily affairs, and share what we have and what we have learned as a nation and practice what we have learned. America can become a world leader by example rather than by show of force. If we had to tell the truth about our motives for going into another country with military force, it is unlikely that our government would be allowed to spend the lives of our youth for the economic gain of the power structure. It is unlikely that prejudice would thrive in a nation where individuals confronted their own fear rather than compensating by diminishing others. It is unlikely that a nation guided by a Spiritual Source would take lightly the needs of humankind.

We can create an America that is strong, powerful, benevolent, caring, and compassionate. We can create an America that puts the well-being of its people before the gain of a minority of power addicts. America can actually become the America that its Impostor has pretended it to be. When human concerns and spiritual values can be the primary goal of America, we are then, as a nation, Life Masters. This Life Mastery will be a reflection of our personal Mastery and our world visions. As society progresses toward Mastery, we each will be able to make a contribution to this process.

Confronting Our National History

The history of America as I learned it in school was a complete fiction. It was about as grounded in reality as the Bible and was used for the same purpose; to create the impression of rightness and virtuousness and to cover up the naked need for control and power. I was an adult before I knew that black history was part of American history or that blacks had a culture before slavery. That creates a kind of slavery. American history is written to support a myth about what America is. What America is the land of the rich and the home of our shame.

Jim Reginald, *Newark, 1989*

JIM REGINALD IS AN ACTIVIST, AND HAS BEEN ALL OF HIS ADULT LIFE. He is an iconoclast who wanted to find a legacy to leave his children besides the poverty that had been passed on to him and the culture of drugs that he had picked up in his own youth on the streets. He wanted his children to grow up proud and concerned. In order to do that he had to teach his own children their history.

He wanted them to learn that their country had done them wrong and that it was all right to want more than was being offered to them as African Americans. He wanted to teach them that his people had been excluded historically and systematically from the bounties that are the promise of America. He wanted his children to know that though there are laws to protect them, history has provided fertile ground for their persecution and poverty. Jim taught his children that they must know the truth in order to overcome this history and the way it is reflected in the present. They must know that the deck is stacked and demand a full hand to play with.

Just like Jim's children, and no matter what our race, we must cut through the denial that insists that anything we have ever done as a nation has been right and done for the right reasons. Only then can we master our national history. This means that we must allow our national shame to come to the surface. We must face that shame in order to stop repeating our shameful behavior. We are a shame-based nation. We have committed atrocities against other people in the name of patriotism, in the name of God, and in the name of righteousness.

In order to maintain the illusion of our rightness, we have told history as a series of fairy tales that always have happy endings. In these fairy tales there is always some thing, some place, or some principle in danger that we, the American prince, are charged to rescue. What we do not reveal in the telling of these myths are the real reasons for our involvement, the real reasons for the spilling of blood.

The story of America's discovery has forever been told as if the Europeans who stumbled mistakenly upon our shores while trying to reach India were noble and daring do-gooders looking for a place to turn into paradise. The truth is that despots and rakes escaping the law and other responsibilities came here to rape the land and kill its occupants. We treated the native people of our land in a criminal manner. We then robbed them of their history so that we would not taint ours. The truth about these events is just now becoming prominent and has yet to find its way into the history that we teach in school.

If you were to read the Declaration of Independence without being told what it was, you might think it a radical document. The instigators of the American Revolution were indeed radical in their outlook and committed to freedom. The framers of the Constitution, however—though many of them were the same men who drafted the Declaration of Independence—were suddenly the winners of the spoils of war. The Constitution was created to preserve and protect the rights of land-owning, monied white men. The radicals of the Revolution became the conservators of their own personal system—a system that would enslave generations to come. Equal rights were never intended for people of color, women, or any other minority group. The former rebels were now the elite and all others were subject to their rules. Only the Bill of Rights—an afterthought to the Constitution—offered any safety from the tyranny of those who would impose their will and a covertly dysfunctional national system upon others.

Denial and a shroud of lies permitted the systematic destruction of the Native Americans and the enslavement of the black race imported to our shores. The Civil War is always portrayed as a noble effort on the part of the North to free the slaves. In truth, there were many economic factors that motivated involvement. Then, as now, racism was as real in the North as it was in the South. Though we are no longer have lynch mobs, a metaphoric lynching continues today, in more subtle but no less dysfunctional forms of persecution.

In foreign wars America has left a trail of blood and destruction that has greatly outweighed any moral justification that we can come up with. Even our involvement in World War II was not entirely altruistic. There were two other reasons: we were attacked and we needed some way to get ourselves out of an economic depression. We waited a very long time to do battle with the tyrants of fascism and national socialism.

Our presence in Southeast Asia has been dubious, and had some disastrous effects. The military-industrial complex, which General Dwight Eisenhower warned us about, allowed the national well-being to be subverted to espionage and denial, a classic example of the dysfunctional model on a grand scale. The invasions of Vietnam and Cambodia were all part of a national disgrace that was marketed as a national calling.

The need to always be right, to deny anything that casts aspersions on our rightness, and to blame and abuse anyone who threatens to upset the myth of national sainthood—all that is a replication of the denial and no-talk rules that keep family secrets. No one is allowed to say that Daddy is a drunk or that the government has ever been run by racketeers and business cartels.

America has habitually lived in opposition to some real or imagined enemy. When the Cold War ended and the red menace could no longer be used to justify the money that has been poured into defense, we came up with a hot war. Since we have habitually done business with despots if it's been profitable, we created Saddam Hussein, but he developed a mind of his own so we turned him into the enemy, thus showing the world that we needed to maintain our military might. Though we declared victory and acted as if we were a nation that had just saved the world, the truth is that the tyrant was left in power, secure with his weaponry, a national hero who left behind burning oil fields in Kuwait, further damaging our already fragile global environment. The winning of this war was a public-relations trick. It took monumental national denial to watch the truth on television and not see it.

With the same blind eye that allows us to watch the ethnic cleansing in the former Yugoslavia on television, we ignore the homeless, ignore the plight of the underclass, and wage an unsuccessful war on drugs rather than see that the quality of life in our country is what drives our kids to drugs.

As I write this we are well into the second decade of the AIDS crisis. This is the first disease in the history of the world whose spread can be directly traced to apathy and fundamentalism, not to mention the hideous possibility that AIDS might have become a solution to some of the world's problems with hunger, poverty, and overpopulation. George Bush claimed to be the leader of the world's most powerful nation, but he failed to take the lead in the war against AIDS. Education has not been mandated to prevent the spread of this disease to our children. Where money was allocated, fraudulent figures and false promises replaced actual funding. Red tape replaced adequate research, and conservatism let a million of our own men, women, and children become infected.

Everywhere we turn there are vivid examples of global and national dysfunction. In the face of all we know, there is no excuse for the raping of the environment for the profit of industry. The rain forest should be sacred. Nuclear power plants should be closed. It is absurd to create more nuclear waste until we know how to get rid of it safely. Our water sources should be off-limits to chemicals that will rob future generations of life. Profiteers have created a false conflict between job security and environmental protection; there is no conflict, only tunnel vision and an incredible lack of vision. It is inexcusable that we are leaving the bill for the greed of the present powers that be as a legacy to future generations.

All of the issues that we have looked at are but individual symptoms of global dysfunction run riot. Will run riot. Greed run riot. They are symptoms of the low level of consciousness and the high level of greed that have been passed down from generation to generation without thought of the consequences. We have lived as if our actions do not have ramifications, just as this reflects the inability of dysfunctional individuals to be responsible for the ramifications of their behavior in the lives of those around them.

As we have seen, this dysfunction is not terminal. There is hope. There is transformation. There is recovery. We can change ourselves and we can change society.

Some of our national denial began to crumble when the rotten core of our society was finally exposed, and quite boldly, too, in the form of the Republican National Convention of 1992. What was revealed was a core of prejudice, sexism, racism, homophobia, and narrow-minded hatred. In the midst of the horror there was a moment of hope when my friend Mary Fisher, a mother and artist with HIV, addressed the convention with great courage, and enormous grace. We as a nation had elected a head of state who condoned such hatefulness and allowed it to represent his party and the nation. The difference between an abusive head of household and an abusive head of state lies only in the number of people who must suffer the consequences of his or her dysfunction. If we are to recover we must pay close attention to reality, as a nation.

The national attention is very hard to grab. We are so determined to maintain our image that the light of truth makes us angry. We often condemn the voices of those who shout in our faces and remind us that we have work to do. As our national amnesia lifts and we face the reality of the society that we have created, we can shift to clarity. Even though there is a new administration, a new wave, and a new chance, it is still our responsibility to do our share of the shifting. Throughout our dysfunctional history, there have been many individuals who have been following a path of real growth, with deep concern for the issues that plague us as a nation and as a planet. And there are those who have stood outside the system and shouted truths in our collective consciousness.

There have been those who have transcended the jargon and star worship of the New Age and psychosocial pop movements and followed their own Spiritual Source into the very real world. These individuals have transcended their egos enough to be part of a movement to tell the truth about who we are as a society.

There are many who have brought awareness to the world at risk to their own security. Ralph Nader told consumers that they had rights. Betty Friedan and Gloria Steinem, among others, risked everything to tell women that they had rights and that responsibility goes with those rights. Shirley MacLaine went out on a limb to bring metaphysics into the mainstream. Producer Howard Rosenman demonstrated the spiritual possibilities to us in such films as *Resurrection*, one of the first pictures to look at the world of metaphysical healing, and *Common Threads*, which tells the story of the AIDS Memorial Quilt. Elisabeth Kübler-Ross and Stephen and Ondrea Levine have challenged our fears around death and dying in the most gentle, nurturing manner possible. Jesse Jackson created economic and political empowerment in the black community by setting a powerful role model with Operation PUSH. Oprah Winfrey has made us aware of child abuse, and of how a powerful women can make things happen and be a role model for others. Elizabeth Taylor has made it possible to raise money and consciousness around AIDS. And the list goes on.

We are most familiar with these celebrities and others such as Whoopi Goldberg, Ted Danson, Judith Light, and hundreds of other stars who use their fame as a vehicle for changing consciousness, but there are literally thousands upon thousands of individuals in all walks of public and private life who risk their security and comfort for a greater good. These people are just human beings with the willingness to lead the way to growth and awareness. They have helped to reawaken consciousness on a grass-roots level that it is time to shift national priorities and concerns. As America shifts the way it perceives itself, there is a realization that the greater good needs to take precedent over personal aggrandizement and that only unity can create true recovery (another twelve-step principle).

Those who cried *no* in the face of the way it has always been have exposed our national shame. Only when we tell the truth about this shame and begin to make choices that reveal the whole truth of our past can we be free of it. Only when we can see the patterns that we have followed throughout our history can we break them, and make choices that will bring us out of our cycle of repetitive addiction to power. Only by allowing our historic vulnerability to surface can we create an atmosphere for changing the rules that have run our government policies and systems. When we follow the example of the unreasonable people who have already brought change and enlightenment to our society, we can look forward to helping create a new world based in possibility and humanity.

Whole Living as a Nation

We know more as a nation than we did. There's a pull
to recognize the importance of human dignity and human
values. We have a chance to be very powerful in a very
different way. Not militarily powerful, but internally
powerful.

Paul Kawata, *Washington, D.C., 1992*

IMAGINE A NEW AMERICA WHERE UNIQUENESS IS HONORED, WHERE
SPONTANEITY COMES NATURALLY, WHERE EACH INDIVIDUAL IS ENCOURAGED
AND SUSTAINED, WHERE DIVERSITY IS WELCOMED AND SUPPORTED. Imagine
that your race, your ethnic origin, your sexuality, your spiritual per-
suasion, are all granted equal rights without question. Imagine each of
us being valued simply as a human being, not because we are the *right*
kind of human being. Imagine an America that honors other nations
in their uniqueness rather than trying to make them reflect its own
image.

Imagine an America that would respond with spontaneity to events
and circumstances, both internally and globally. As each incident
arose, we would treat it in the context of the present moment, allowing
the governmental system to support the needs of the moment rather
than forcing our response to fit the system.

Imagine a kind of national Whole Living where emotions are
honored, recognized, and expressed freely. There is a sign outside the
entrance to the United States Senate that states, "There will be no
displays of emotion in the Senate Chamber." That statement would be
considered a national disgrace in a truly functional New America.
Imagine that we are a nation of people who express themselves, have
permission to grieve, permission to be joyous, and permission, as a
nation, to present ourselves as diversified but not divided.

Imagine an America where the truth is told. Imagine an America where we feel no national shame; where we would not need to make it look as if we all think alike; where as a nation, we do not need the agreement of other nations to validate our position; where we would not be threatened by another point of view, political position, or system of government; where we could allow other nations to thrive, to be autonomous, and to express their own worldviews.

Imagine a truly empowered America. Since power includes vulnerability, the United States would not need to have control over the rest of the world. We could be partners with other powerful nations and not perceive their power as a threat. If we could allow ourselves to be vulnerable, we could be supported by other powerful and rich nations. Given a powerful alliance, we would be able to give up our job as watchdog superhero of the planet. This does not mean that we become weak or let others hurt us. This does not mean that we cannot go to the aid of a colleague nation, if invited. What it means is that in a new America we are not run by the fear of other nations' power. We invite their power.

Imagine that as a nation we would honor both the physical and psychological boundaries of other nations. We wouldn't invade the borders of others. We would be secure within our own space and identity, which would not be determined by the issues of other nations. Our integrity would not be subverted by the chance to make money or destroy a differing point of view. Our view of ourselves and our national self-worth would not depend on our status as a world dictator. Our role in the world would be flexible and respectful.

Imagine that in this new America, we were allowed to make mistakes. They would be considered things that we did, not viewed as our national identity. Our mistakes could be viewed as learning experiences that would guide us in future circumstances. It would also be assumed that we would continue to make mistakes, because this New America is made up of human beings. But we would be able to admit these mistakes rather than create dysfunctional national cover-ups, and make amends to those whom we've harmed.

This means that a new America would be accountable for its actions, but without blame. Imagine that we would be responsible for our own feelings, our word, and our communication. In other words, as a nation, we would behave in an adult manner, free from the childish need always to be right, always to find an outside source to blame for our internal troubles. We would keep our word, say what we mean, and mean what we say.

Lastly, imagine an America with the freedom to be fully itself and available for intimacy. This would mean that America would be the big, joyous melting pot it has always pretended to be. We could be quirky, eccentric, a collection of many cultures, many spiritual points of view, and tapped into our Spiritual Source enough to be close to other nations without posturing.

All of this is possible. All of this could be easily obtainable with enough vision and enough willingness to shift the way we operate as individuals and as a nation. With such new national awareness, we can look to see what shape we want to bring to this new America and how the principles of Whole Living can be applied to all aspects of society. We can imagine—and create—an America that is Masterful.

National Mastery

Can you imagine what would happen if everyone in government went through a process that dealt with their personal issues or had to be in some sort of program? Picture members of Congress having to spend a weekend together discovering that they had plenty in common, like the pain of growing up and the dysfunction that they function in. They might even discover that they have the same job—which is supposed to be taking care of the quality of life for us!

John Denissen, *Santa Fe, 1991*

IT IS IMPOSSIBLE TO CHANGE SOCIETY WITHOUT SHIFTING THE EXPERIENCE OF ITS INDIVIDUALS. Life Mastery is available when you shift your perception of who you are from the Impostor to your Genuine Self. If we are to do this as a nation, it is critical that as many influential people as possible experience this shift. Then the nation might shift too.

I work within many health-care institutions. As health care changes form in this country, the system must expand and transform itself to accommodate the needs of society. I start by working on a personal level with groups of hospital personnel, expanding to work with the whole institution. Shifting the experience of individuals ultimately improves the quality of the service and management of the institution.

What usually happens is that the greater purpose of an institution—as well as those within it—becomes lost in the struggle to survive the system. The members of a hospital staff and administration alike are thrown together and suddenly see that they all have a shared experience of the systems that they grew up in and the systems in which they work. Since all of them are programmed to play their roles by their personal histories, too often they are kept from seeing the real job. The real job for them is health care and their own emotional health.

It works like this. We are attracted to jobs for different reasons. Some of the reasons have to do with the work itself; the satisfaction, the use of skills, the opportunity to express the things one cares about, to serve. But we are also attracted to our chosen fields for other, less nurturing, reasons. For many, basic need plays a great role—the need for power, prestige, to be needed, to be noticed. For many, the issues of work or service become entangled with personal needs and expectations. For many, the unresolved issues of childhood run riot over present reality.

Once you can recognize the distinctions between these areas of your life, you can handle the real issues of your job, whether you are a nurse, the director of a hospital, or a United States senator. You can handle your personal issues at home and with the appropriate people, and you can handle your unresolved childhood issues in therapy or appropriate programs. What is lacking in most cases are the communication skills and tools to differentiate one area of your life from the other.

The mission of hospitals is health care. It has long been a goal to transform and shift not only the way individual hospitals work, but the health-care system itself. Just as transforming the quality of experience for individuals transforms the way the hospital operates and the quality of care that it offers, so could the transformation of many hospitals within a given city transform health care within that city. This can be carried to a national level.

Imagine Congress operating in a Masterful way, free of the influence of personal dramas and childhood traumas. Imagine your Senate and your House of Representatives exploring their personal needs together so that the barriers between them—and their partisanship—could slip away, for their own good and the greater good. What if each member individually traveled down a long corridor, as you did in the first visualization in this book, and discovered the source of his or her dysfunction and needs? What if these legislators discovered the rules that they set up in childhood and how those rules affect their ability to govern as well as their own well-being?

Imagine every senator and representative actually standing up for the needs of his or her constituency. Imagine them being flexible and supporting the greater good and coming up with creative solutions to local issues that might require their constituents to give something up for that greater purpose. Imagine the people who represent you being so clear of the prejudice and needs and lies of their childhood that they could be present purely to do their jobs.

Imagine that everyone in your local government—and every bureaucrat in every department that serves the public interest—had to explore his or her own well-being in order to serve yours. This would certainly change the way things worked. The idea, though fantastic, raises the concept of personal and public satisfaction as a priority. We are a nation that has embraced recovery on a large scale among individuals. Why not on a grander scale? I know that it is possible to take the personal work that we do and expand it to work in institutions. I've seen it work with hospital staffs and I've seen it save the sanity of agencies working in nonprofit causes. Why not government?

We are a nation in recovery. That recovery will depend upon the participation of each individual. It will also depend on future generations. Imagine what it would be like to bring up a generation that did not need to recover. Imagine that life skills, and Whole Life skills, were taught in the public schools. Imagine shifting the entire educational system to reflect the needs of real children in contemporary society. Imagine that the system served the needs of our children rather than forcing children to fit into an archaic system.

First of all, though teachers are a noble breed, there are many who suffer greatly from their own dysfunction, abuse, and need for control. This is true of those who run the schools, sit on school boards, and design programs. There are many dedicated, creative visionaries involved in education. In order that they take their places at the head of the movement for better education, they too must face their personal and childhood issues, and be prepared to create a system that acknowledges the reality of society.

In areas where kids stand little chance of having the American dream, early education is a great place to begin telling that truth. In this way, children can prepare themselves for an uphill battle. In the light of this truth they can begin to make choices that will serve their lives rather than take drugs to make life bearable.

This brings me to one of the main problems with our educational system—or any system that we create to replace it. It doesn't matter if you teach by rote learning, cognitive methods, or experientially—if children are afraid to go home, they cannot do homework. If their minds are occupied with survival, they cannot learn to read. If they are abused, even a nonabusive school system will not prepare them for learning, let alone life.

Schools need to be safe zones. Teachers need to be aware of their own childhood issues and transcend any discomfort in order to offer shelter to the children of our lost society. What if all that we know about recovery could be injected right into the education system? It could work if the most basic skill that was taught was whole and functional communication. There should be no fear generated in children by teachers or teaching institutions. Fear has never engendered respect or good behavior. Fear replicates home dysfunction too closely for most children.

Children need to know that they are not alone in their suffering, abuse, feelings of alienation, and shame. If there could be time, safe time each day, set aside for children of all ages to talk freely, share and get support, life in school would be different. Such an atmosphere would create a fertile ground for learning, and growth and healthier people in an ever healthier nation.

Life Mastery and Personal Vision

The thing that keeps me going is using what I know *about myself to help other people. The other thing is that I really give a damn about what happens in the world. I know that while I am still able I can do what it takes to wake people up. It makes me sad that it is taking so long for people to get it but I won't give up.*

Terry Sutton, *San Francisco, 1988*

IF LIFE MASTERY IS A POSSIBILITY ON A GLOBAL SCALE IT IS ONLY SO BE-CAUSE YOU HAVE MASTERED WHOLE LIVING AND CAN CONTRIBUTE TO THE HEAL-ING OF AMERICA AND TO MAKING THE WORLD A BETTER PLACE TO LIVE IN. This doesn't mean that you have to quit your life and run for office. It doesn't mean that you have to enroll your congresspeople in a twelve-step program or make your local school board and teachers do a seminar. What it does mean is that you can begin to treat public people in a manner that reflects what you know about Mastery and Whole Living.

If, for example, you care for the environment, you can participate in its care in many ways, from recycling to becoming a "green" candidate. You can speak out among your friends or you can organize the constituents of your representatives in government to pressure them to serve the environment. You may participate in the expansion of our national vision and creativity to find a way to make economic profit and environmental concerns work hand in glove. There are examples all through the world of business where this is possible. Look at The Body Shop, a small, environmentally correct attempt at beauty care that has turned into a major multinational business. Look at how chic and profitable it is to use and sell recycled paper or eat Ben and Jerry's natural ice cream. Surely we can make profits and jobs by turning war research and production into peace research and production. People who cut down trees can build up something else. There is no discrepancy between good works and good incomes.

If your passion is directed toward the issues of the homeless you can give a dollar to someone in need or you can help build a house for Habitat for Humanity. You can throw a fund-raiser or work to make your city provide for the homeless. You can help create a safe shelter. There are a million ways that you, just you, can contribute.

AIDS, the environment, civil liberties, nuclear waste, education, literacy, world hunger, and an enormous list of other worthy causes are out there. They are all calling for your attention. Your consciousness is important. Working on any piece of this whole, in any way, will help to bring light to the rest. You and all the other Masterful individuals have within you a vision for how you would like to see the world and your place in it.

I believe that when we were small we had a very strong sense of our ability to move mountains. I also think that no matter how self-deprecating and frightened you may have been in your lifetime, there has always been, living beneath the surface, a powerful vision and a sense that you were indeed powerful. I have found in working with people in unfolding their personal vision that for many, their vision is so huge that they are embarrassed. For others it is so small that they are embarrassed. No matter the size, each personal vision is important.

If you are to best serve, and experience rapture in return, you need to discover where your passion lies. It is not possible to work on all fronts, so you must be clear what your vision for the world is and what place you hold. You can influence the lives of the people directly around you and the systems within which you operate. The scope of your vision does not matter. What matters is that once you are in touch with your Genuine Self and your vision, you are able to move others. For most of you, your personal vision has been there all along.

Breathe through your body.
Begin to be very aware of your feelings.
Let out a sound.
Begin to see a brilliant light in your heart center.
Let that light radiate through you.

Let it radiate through you and beyond.
Let it fill your field of vision.

In this field of light begin to see an image of yourself.
See yourself as Masterful.
Let yourself experience the love and compassion that you have
  for yourself . . .
Let the feelings fill you.
Now go over to that image and embrace it, bringing it into you,
  inside your body, so that you are one.

Begin to be aware of yourself in a vast, empty space.
Begin to allow into that space everything that
  you have ever dreamed you could have or have ever wanted.
Allow yourself to experience yourself surrounded by all the people
  you have ever dreamed that you might have in your life.
See yourself in the relationships and doing the things
  that have always been your wildest dreams and most powerful
  wishes.
Take your time and let things just show up . . .
Let them fill your field of vision, flood your senses, overpower you
  with joy.
Have it all.
Have it now.
Experience yourself living life to the fullest . . .
Let your imagination run wild.
Bring in more.
Let it get better and better, more fulfilling than you ever thought
  possible!
Don't let any voices from the past inhibit the scope of your im-
  agination.
Don't let history limit your desire or deserving.

. . .

Begin to see yourself with others.
See the effect that you can have on others.
Let your fantasies run wild.
Let yourself experience how powerful your reflection can be.
See how your ability to let life be wonderful moves others.
See them grow in self-love as you do.
Deeply feel the effect of that love.
No restrictions.
See your effect on them.
See yourself in service to them.
What can you do for them?
Let your imagination run free . . .

Begin to see the world around you the way you know that it
* could be.*
See it the way your imagination can create it.
See the world as Whole . . .
See your place in it . . .
See how you have helped to influence it, to shape it, to
* empower it.*
What did you do?
How did you contribute?
What area of need did you fill?
Let your imagination stretch . . .
What were you so passionate about that you were moved to
* action?*
What did you do?
Who did you work with?
Feel the power of it.
See the effect!

. . .

Now begin to let this vision expand!

Let your fantasies run free.

How wonderful can you envision the world, the universe?

What's your place in it?

Just allow yourself to be immersed in your ultimate fantasy
*   for yourself and the world.*

Allow yourself to experience it as real!

Feel it in your body.

Now allow it to become even more powerful, more wonderful . . .

Take your time and savor this experience . . .

Know that you have played a great part in making this vision a
*   reality.*

See yourself in the midst of this ultimate vision for the planet,
*   the universe!*

Allow brilliant light to radiate everywhere!

In that light see a small child.

Let the child approach you and hear it ask you
*   how you were able to manifest this vision.*

What did you do?

How did you begin?

How did you get from where you were to this vision?

From where you sat when you became moved by your vision,
*   to where you are now?*

What was the first step?

Now hear yourself speak to the child.

Tell the child what your part was, so simply that the child will
*   understand.*

How was it for you?

Take your time.

Be simple.

Be clear.
Let yourself tell the child and listen to your words.
You know how to make it happen.
You know what it would take to have your vision become a
  reality.
Deep within you.
You know your power.
You know your place in the scheme of things.
Let the words flow and breathe them through your body.
Take your time, and when you understand, ask the child
   if there are any other questions.
See what else is needed.
When you have given all of the information that you have to offer,
  embrace the child and allow the image to fade.

Just see yourself there with your vision, with your light.
Know that it is real, it is yours.
With vision, life becomes an adventure of the spirit,
   the heart, and the body.
You have within you the vision to be creative.
You have within you the vision to participate
   in the transformation of life on earth.
You have much to give and much to gain.
You are part of a greater whole, an integral and important part
  of blessed spirit.
You are the real, practical manifestation of spirit.
You can put one foot in front of another
   and allow the universe to flow through you.
Your vision is a gift and pleasure to bring into reality.

Remember when you were a daydreaming, imaginative kid? That
quality lives within you. Vision and fantasy are very close. Today's

fantasy can be tomorrow's reality. Many of us turn our fantasies into dreams. Others turn them into reality. That is the difference between a dreamer and a visionary. A visionary will act on his or her dreams. I do not mean to imply that everyone must be out on the front lines. Those who must, will, and the rest of us can still be Masters in the world we inhabit. As long as you hold your vision and hold a sense that you are but a part of a greater whole, then everything you do can become an expression of that vision.

Your well-being is part of that vision. It doesn't take giving up your life as you know it and going off to distant lands to participate in healing the planet. It has more to do with living out of personal integrity and moving others with your love. It has more to do with reflecting your spirit through everything you do. It has to do with allowing your life to reflect your Genuine Self and being a responsible and conscious citizen of the world. Once you know who you are, you can do no less.

If it can happen to enough of us, then the earth will no longer reflect dysfunction. It will reflect love and worth and power. The tragic history of the planet will no longer inform the present.

We are global. The more that you live a life of love and Mastery, the more you know that you are a part of the global community. When you live Masterfully you can shift from being part of the global problem to being part of the global solution. As individuals and as individuals together we can live Whole, productive lives—lives that are full of love—lives in which our Genuine Selves are Masters.

Index